Gender Budgets Make More Cents

Country Studies and Good Practice

Debbie Budlender and Guy Hewitt

Commonwealth Secretariat

Gender Section
Commonwealth Secretariat
Marlborough House
Pall Mall, London SW1Y 5HX
UNITED KINGDOM

Email: gad@commonwealth.int
http://www.thecommonwealth.org/gender
http://www.gender-budgets.org

Published by the Commonwealth Secretariat

Layout & design by Pen and Ink
Printed by Formara Ltd.

Copies of this publication can be ordered from:
The Publications Manager, Communications and Public Affairs Division,
Commonwealth Secretariat, Marlborough House, Pall Mall, London,
SW1Y 5HX, UK
Tel. +44 (0) 20 7747 6342
Fax. +44 (0) 20 7839 9081

Email. r.jones-parry@commonwealth.int

ISBN: 0-85092-734-X

Price: £9.99

Publication Team

Contributing Editors: Debbie Budlender and Guy Hewitt

Contributors: Ngone Diop-Tine, Rona Fitzgerald, Celia Flor, Morag Gillespie, Janine Hicks, Helena Hofbauer, Andrea Lizares-Si, Ailsa McKay, Angela O'Hagan, Rebecca Pearl, Donna St. Hill, Marian Sawer, Yoon Jung Sook and Lisa Vetten

Publications Editor: Tina Johnson

Contents

List of Tables

Foreword

At their meeting in September this year, the Commonwealth Finance Ministers will discuss gender-responsive budget (GRB) initiatives. For the first time, a group of finance ministers have agreed to include, as a specific agenda item, gender concerns as they relate to macroeconomics and development. This is a significant step in the process of advancing gender equality.

The willingness of Commonwealth Finance Ministers to explore the relevance and application of these initiatives to government budgets is a testimony of the value of gender budget work and the role of the Commonwealth in its development and promotion. This accessible book will prove extremely useful for those interested in learning more about GRB initiatives.

This publication builds on the previous work, *Gender Budgets Make Cents,* which provided an overview of GRB initiatives, the framework, evolution and lessons learned. This companion title was compiled in response to the need to share 'good practice' in gender budget work based on the documentation and detailed analysis of country studies. The depth and quality of information contained in these chapters will be of immerse value to anyone interested in implementing or strengthening existing gender budget work.

The development of the Commonwealth Secretariat's work in this area has been the product of a collaborative effort among a number of important actors whom I would like to recognise.

Commonwealth governments deserve much credit for their support of GRB initiatives, primarily Finance and Women's Ministers who have provided the leadership. There is also a need to recognise the outstanding work of civil society organisations, many of which have been the catalysts for gender budget work at the country level. By engaging these different actors, this programme exemplifies the call in the 2002 Commonwealth Heads of Government Coolum Communiqué for stronger links between Commonwealth governments, civil society and NGOs. In a world of decreasing resources and increasing need, the partnership between the Commonwealth Secretariat, International Development Research Centre and the United Nations Development Fund for Women, and collaboration with a number of other agencies including the Asian Development

Bank, Pacific Islands Forum, the Southern African Development Community and the United Nations Development Programme has been crucial to the growth and expansion of this programme.

I would like to thank those who have contributed to this publication: Ngone Diop-Tine, Rona Fitzgerald, Celia Flor, Morag Gillespie, Janine Hicks, Helena Hofbauer, Tina Johnson, Andrea Lizares-Si, Ailsa McKay, Angela O'Hagan, Rebecca Pearl, Donna St. Hill, Marian Sawer, Yoon Jung Sook and Lisa Vetten. Many will appreciate, as I have, the sharing of your diverse experiences. Finally, I feel it necessary to acknowledge separately the efforts of Debbie Budlender and Guy Hewitt, a dynamic duo whom I consider central to the future of GRB initiatives in the Commonwealth and beyond.

Nancy Spence
Director, Social Transformation Programmes Division
Commonwealth Secretariat

Abbreviations

ADB	Asian Development Bank
AER	Annual Expenditure Report
BBC	British Broadcasting Corporation
BCWO	Bacolod Consortium of Women's Organizations
CASE	Community Agency for Social Enquiry
CDC	City Development Council
CEPEX	Commission of the Ministry of Finance
CGE	Commission on Gender Equality
CIQLFW	Committee on the Improvement of the Quality of Life and Status of Women
COINS	Constraints, options, incentives and needs
CONAMU	National Council of Women
CRE	Commission for Racial Equality
CSG	Consultative Steering Group
CSVR	Centre for the Study of Violence and Reconciliation
CTC	Child Tax Credit
DAWN	Development Through Active Women Networking Foundation
DFID	UK Department for International Development
DILG	Department of Interior and Local Government
DSSD	Department of Social Services and Development
EEO	Equal employment opportunity
EOC	Equal Opportunities Commission
EPBAG	Equality Proofing Budgets Advisory Group
EQUIDAD	Equidad de Género, Ciudadanía, Trabajo y Familia
EWBG	Engender Women's Budget Group
FCS	Family Violence, Child Protection and Sexual Offences
FEPOMUVES	Women's Popular Federation
FORO	Foro Nacional de Mujeres y Políticas de Población
GAD	Gender and Development
GAP	Gender Advocacy Programme
GBI	Gender Budget Initiative
GDI	Gender and Development Index

GDP	gross domestic product
GETNET	Gender Education and Training Network
GNP	gross national product
GRB	Gender-Responsive Budget
GTZ	Deutsche Gessellschaft für Technische Zusammenarbeit (German Technical Cooperation Agency)
HDI	Human Development Index
IAFFE	International Association for Feminist Economics
IDRC	International Development Research Centre
ICPD	International Conference on Population and Development
IPU	Inter-Parliamentary Union
IRA	Internal Revenue Allotment
LGU	Local Government Unit
MILENIO	Milenio Feminista
MIGEPROFE	Ministry of Gender and Women in Development
MINECOFIN	Ministry of Finance and Economic Planning
MOOE	Maintenance and other operating expenses
MP	Member of Parliament
MPL	Member of the Provincial Legislature
MSP	Member of the Scottish Parliament
MTEF	Medium Term Expenditure Framework
NGO	Non-governmental organisation
NSO	National Statistics Office
OECD	Organisation of Economic Cooperation and Development
OSW	Office of the Status of Women
PAC	Programa de Ampliación de Cobertura
PAHO	Pan American Health Organization
PAN	Partido Acción Nacional
PIP	Public investment programme
PCW	Provincial Council for Women
PoA	Commonwealth Plan of Action on Gender and Development
PPP	Provincial Parliamentary Programme
PRI	Partido Revolucionario Institucional

PROGRESA	Programa de Educación, Salud y Alimentación,
PRSP	Poverty Reduction Strategy Paper
PWC	Parliamentary Women's Caucus
SADC	Southern African Development Community
SACTWU	Southern African Clothing and Textile Workers Union
TAF	The Asia Foundation
UNDAW	United Nations Division for the Advancement of Women
UNDP	United Nations Development Programme
UNIFEM	United Nations Development Fund for Women
UNFPA	United Nations Population Fund
WBG	Women's Budget Group
WBI	Women's Budget Initiative
WEDO	Women's Environment and Development Organization
WEU	Women and Equality Unit
WHO	World Health Organization
WNC	Women's National Commission

Introduction

Debbie Budlender and Guy Hewitt

This book builds on a previous publication, *Gender Budgets Makes Cents*. The earlier work provided an overview of gender-responsive budget (GRB) initiatives.[1] It described the conceptual framework, evolution of the work and lessons learned. It also provided brief summaries of country initiatives. This book is a response to the need to document 'good practice' in gender budget work from across the globe. For the first time, it provides easy access to detailed country information and analysis on the why, where and how of gender-responsive budgets.

We choose to talk about 'good practice' rather than 'best practice' for two reasons. Firstly, at this point in time no country in the world has achieved a completely gender-responsive budget. Some countries are further along the road to reaching that goal than others, but none has reached it yet. Secondly, the term 'best practice' might suggest that there is a single, 'best' way in which gender budget work should be done. One of the strongest messages of this book, however, is that how one tackles gender budget work must be strongly influenced by the political, economic, social and cultural situation in a country. There is no single blueprint, or recipe, for successful gender budget work. The chapter on the Andean region, for example, which gives examples of initiatives in three countries, reveals some of the differences that can emerge both between and within countries even when initiatives form part of a single project.

The book contains ten stories of engagement in gender budget work. Most of the chapters tell the story of work in a single country. The exceptions are the Andean chapter mentioned above and the chapter on the Commonwealth Secretariat, which looks at how this international agency has attempted to promote gender budget work among its members.

All but one of the chapters focus on work which is ongoing. At

---

[1] The term 'gender-responsive budget' is increasingly being adopted as the standard name for a variety of processes which have been hitherto referred to as 'applied gender budget analysis', 'gender-sensitive budgets', 'gender budgets' and 'women's budgets'.

present there are over 50 countries in the world where there have been gender budget initiatives of some kind. However, some of these initiatives involve one-off activities. Others are relatively dormant at present. For this reason, we chose to focus on countries where there is currently significant activity. The exception is the chapter on Australia which is included because, although it looks primarily at developments from the mid-1990s, this was the first country to engage in gender budget work.

We also, for the most part, chose countries whose stories are not well known. These choices mean, firstly, that we have omitted several countries where significant activity has occurred, but whose stories have been told several times. These include Tanzania and Uganda. Secondly, the South African chapter, rather than retelling the story of the first years of that country's initiative, describes the latest activities, while the Philippines chapter focuses on recent non-governmental organisation (NGO) activity at local government level rather than the government's institutionalised gender and development (GAD) budget.

While it was not a conscious consideration in choosing case studies, a reading of the chapters reveals that many occurred at a time when the country concerned was undergoing, or had recently undergone, significant change. For example, South Africa's initiative started after the first democratic elections of 1994; Scotland's initiative responded to devolution – the partial political separation from the United Kingdom (UK); the UK's own initiative only truly came of age after Labour's election victory; and Rwanda's initiative is occurring as a new post-genocide government attempts to reconstruct the country.

All the chapters are written by practitioners – by people who are, or have been, actively involved in the activities they describe. This approach has clear benefits in that the writers have first-hand experience and in-depth knowledge. It could, of course, also have disadvantages in that practitioners might be unwilling to describe weaknesses openly, or might simply not see them. We did, however, encourage authors to reflect on both the challenges and successes of their initiatives, and most chapters include a discussion of these aspects. By asking practitioners rather than outside observers to comment, we were also acknowledging that in an ongoing political endeavour such as gender budgets, there are sometimes things that are better left unsaid.

The book provides a relatively wide geographical spread. The experiences described include examples from Africa, Latin America,

East and South-east Asia, Europe and the Pacific. Every chapter
except the one on the Commonwealth Secretariat contains a box of
indicators that give the overall population of the country, the
percentage of the population that is female and that is urban, the gross
domestic product (GDP) per capita in US dollars, the human and
gender development indices (HDI and GDI), the percentage of the total
government budget funded by donors, and the percentage of national
parliamentarians who are women. Unfortunately, several of the
indicators for Scotland were not available as the United Nations
Development Programme's *Human Development Report* includes the
country in a composite measure for the UK. This lack of separate
statistics is particularly interesting given that the Scottish chapter
focuses on the way in which devolution provided the impetus for their
gender budget initiative.

Table 1 below shows the lowest and highest values for each of these
indicators across the countries involved. In terms of size of population
alone, the range is from 5.1 million for Scotland to 79.5 million for
Philippines. In terms of GDP per capita, the range is even larger.
Australia's GDP per capita is more than 32 times that of Rwanda's.
Australia and Rwanda also have the highest and lowest scores
respectively for the HDI and GDI. This is, at least in part, because GDP
per capita is one of the key constituents of these two measures.
Because of its relative poverty, Rwanda is also the country with the
largest proportion of its budget funded by external donors. Korea is the
only country covered in this book which ranks lower for the GDI than
for the HDI. It is also the country with the lowest representation of
women in its national parliament. Further, it is the most rural of the
sample of countries. All these factors, and others, affect the shape of
gender budget initiatives in each country.

Table 1: Lowest and highest indicators across countries included in this book

Indicator	Lowest	Country	Highest	Country
Population	5.1m	Scotland	79.5m	Philippines
% of population which is female	49.8%	Korea	54%	Rwanda
% of population which is urban	9%	Korea	91%	Scotland
Gross domestic product (GDP) per capita (US$)	885	Rwanda	28,433	Australia
Human development index (HDI)	0.395	Rwanda	0.936	Australia
Gender development index (GDI)	0.391	Rwanda	0.935	Australia
% of total budget funded by donors	0%	Several	65%	Rwanda
% of national parliamentarians who are women	6%	Korea	30%	South Africa

Gender budget work can be undertaken by government, by parliament or by civil society. International organisations can also engage, preferably in an enabling or supportive role. The book contains examples of initiatives which involve each of these actors. In some cases these actors are working together. In all cases there is, as one would expect when looking at government budgets, some engagement with government. However, in many cases, for reasons explained by the authors, the main actors are from civil society.

The Australian and Rwandan chapters provide examples of cases where government is the primary actor. The Philippines also has an institutionalised government initiative, but the chapter in this book tells the story of an NGO initiative in that country. Many of the chapters suggest that, while a change in the government budget is the ultimate objective of most initiatives, there are many other gains to be made along the way. In particular, gender budget work is a way of enhancing democracy, civil society participation and accountability.

In briefing authors, we told them that we were looking for the 'story' of what had happened in their initiative, but also some analysis of why a particular strategy and approach were chosen, and what the strengths and weaknesses were. We asked authors to concentrate on what has happened already rather than plans for the future. But we said they could discuss, briefly, what their future plans were, as well as how what actually happened differed from their original plans. We asked them to discuss money issues – where they got funds from for the work, and whether and how participants were paid. We felt that all these aspects were important if others were to learn from what they had done.

Some of the chapters provide brief summaries of results of the research-oriented aspects of the work. For example, the Korean chapter looks at results in one of the local governments studied, the Philippines authors describe their findings in respect of Bacolod City's budget, while the Mexican chapter highlights findings of their research into health and poverty-related funding. The UK and Australian chapters raise some of the theoretical and ideological underpinnings of their approaches, while the Rwandan chapter provides the reporting framework which government is using in its gender budget initiative.

We asked authors to write simply in describing their initiatives. Firstly, the hope is that the book will be read by a wide range of people, including those for whom English is not a first language as well as those who do not have tertiary education. Secondly, successful gender budget work requires an engagement and understanding of technical detail, but also requires, if one is to engage civil society, the ability to explain in simple terms what is being done. Thirdly, while those working on gender budget work must engage with a level of country-specific detail which is important for success in their own work, it should not be confusing to readers unfamiliar with that country's situation.

The variations in style of the chapters as well as the types of activities included reveal the differences in objectives, strategies and audiences of the groups involved. The South African chapter describes a conscious attempt to broaden the audience through the development of workshop materials. The Mexican chapter discusses the challenge of an initiative that brings together technical researchers with women members of a more mass-based organisation. The Australian chapter points to the dangers of paying insufficient attention to a civil society audience.

Most of the chapters focus on expenditure. This reflects the overall bias in gender budget initiatives worldwide. The UK chapter and initiative are an exception in this respect. The chapter explains the reason for this as being the way the budget is presented and understood in the British context. The South African chapter describes work done on customs and excise, but points to the problems experienced in generating interest in advocacy around revenue issues.

Virtually all the chapters describe some activities related to sensitisation of government officials, members of civil society or others as to the importance of looking at budgets from a gender perspective. Sensitisation is clearly important. However, sensitisation alone will have limited impact. The South African chapter records the realisation on the part of an NGO, which is involved in training staff dealing with rape survivors, that changing attitudes is not enough. Changed attitudes need to be accompanied by adequate resources as well as the skills to use them. The Rwandan chapter describes the process through which government officials in that country were both made aware of the need for gender-sensitive budgets and trained to take the approach forward in their daily work.

All the authors work from an understanding that the ultimate aim in gender budget work is to ensure that gender is mainstreamed – that it is taken into account in all parts of the government budget. The chapters reveal, however, that most initiatives do not try to tackle the entire budget at once. In many cases there is a decision to focus on particular sectors or portfolios. In the case of Korea and the Philippines, the focus was largely on gender-targeted expenditure. In Korea this focus was chosen in response to the new Framework Act on Women's Development which led to the establishment of women's focal points, a Women's Fund and women-related policies. In the Philippines, the initiative examined what the local government unit had done to comply with the mandated 5 per cent allocation for gender and development, but also went beyond this to explore what had happened in relation to the remaining 95 per cent of the budget.

We know that each of the case studies could have been expanded far beyond its current length. However, the authors were given limits within which that they had to document their initiatives because we wanted to keep the chapters short to make them more accessible. Some of the chapters only tell part of the story of what has happened in a particular country. We hope that this smorgasbord of ideas will inspire you to take forward gender budget work in your own country and organisation.

The Commonwealth Secretariat: The role of external agencies

Guy Hewitt

Introduction

Gender-responsive budget (GRB) initiatives have caught the attention of the gender and development community. Governments, intergovernmental organisations, development agencies, and civil society groups are promoting the use of such initiatives as a central part of their strategy to advance gender equality. This enthusiasm reflects the varied purposes gender-responsive budgets can serve. These include, among others:

◆ improving the allocation of resources to women;

◆ supporting gender mainstreaming in macroeconomics;

◆ strengthening civil society participation in economic policy making;

◆ enhancing the linkages between economic and social policy outcomes;

◆ tracking public expenditure against gender and development policy commitments; and

◆ contributing to the attainment of the Millennium Development Goals (Budlender et al, 2002: 12).

Although the focus of implementation and analysis of GRB initiatives has been at the country level, there is a need for attention to the role of external agencies. This chapter examines the involvement of the Commonwealth Secretariat in the development and implementation of these initiatives. In so doing, it attempts to identify how external agencies can get involved in work in this area and the role they can play at national, regional and international levels. A useful analysis of the role and challenges of donor involvement in these initiatives can be found in *Global Assessment of Gender-Responsive Budget Initiatives* (Budlender et al, 2002: 91).

There are two qualifications which are relevant to this case study.

First, the Commonwealth Secretariat did not provide support to all the GRB initiatives within the Commonwealth. Many were autonomous, in some cases supported by other agencies. Second, the Commonwealth Secretariat's initial approach in implementing initiatives advocated for a government-led process at the national level. However, a feature of many of the Commonwealth initiatives has been the leading role of civil society.

Commonwealth countries which have sought to implement gender-responsive budgets include Australia, Barbados, Belize, Botswana, Canada, Fiji Islands, India, Kenya, Malawi, Malaysia, Mauritius, Mozambique, Namibia, South Africa, Sri Lanka, St Kitts and Nevis, Tanzania, Uganda, UK, Zambia and Zimbabwe.

Background

The Commonwealth is an association of 54 independent states, working together in areas of common interest. With a total population of 1.7 billion people, the Commonwealth represents a third of the world's population and a third of the membership of the United Nations. One of the features of the Commonwealth is the articulation of a developing countries' perspective.

The Commonwealth has been closely associated with GRB initiatives. This is due in part to the number of initiatives – nearly half of the fifty known to have been implemented – that are from the Commonwealth. Additional factors include:

◆ The Commonwealth Secretariat has been centrally involved in the production of tools, methodology and capacity building materials for this programme area;

◆ The Commonwealth has contributed to the international advocacy for the implementation of GRB initiatives; and

◆ The Commonwealth Secretariat has sought to encourage partnerships and collaboration between agencies interested in supporting work in this area. The most significant outcome of this has been the programme partnership with the International Development Research Centre (IDRC) and the United Nations Development Fund for Women (UNIFEM).

Why Gender–responsive Budgets?

Building on existing strengths

Although some agencies within the international community have sought to be leaders on a broad range of gender and development issues, the Commonwealth Secretariat, due to limited human and financial resources, has concentrated its efforts in specific areas where it has been able to demonstrate a comparative advantage. One such area of advantage has been in encouraging governments to integrate gender into economic policy.

The Commonwealth was, for many years, involved in raising awareness of the impact of macroeconomic policy on women. The 1989 Commonwealth Expert Group *Engendering Adjustment for the 1990s* examined the negative impact on women of inappropriate structural adjustment programmes in the 1980s (Commonwealth Secretariat, 1989: 6). It emphasised the importance of social equity and economic growth as well as efficiency, and recommended the full integration of women into decision-making processes.

The report, endorsed by Commonwealth Heads of Government in the 1991 Ottawa Declaration on Women and Structural Adjustment, included a seven-point programme of action (Commonwealth Secretariat, 1992: 3). This advocacy, along with others, played an important role in getting the Bretton Woods institutions – the International Monetary Fund and especially the World Bank – to begin to review their lending policies and conditionalities from a gender perspective.

This prior work gave the organisation the networks, knowledge base and confidence to again commit to playing a pioneering role in a largely undeveloped and uncharted area. Other agencies have adopted similar strategies of linking gender-responsive budgets to existing institutional capacities. For example, UNIFEM has drawn on its civil society focus to support the work of women's organisations in strengthening economic governance. Similarly, the Inter-Parliamentary Union has incorporated this work into its programming on improving the participation of elected representatives of the people in the budget process.

Responding to an enabling environment

The existence of an enabling environment was significant to the Commonwealth's work. The GRB programme was supported by the 1995 Commonwealth Plan of Action on Gender and Development (POA) which was endorsed by Commonwealth Heads of Government as a reaffirmation of their commitment to gender equality as a fundamental value of the Commonwealth.

Many agencies now have operational policy statements on gender and development. The main thrust for the majority is gender mainstreaming. Gender-responsive budgets were seen as an important tool for achieving this. The synergies between GRB initiatives and gender mainstreaming were apparent from the onset. GRB initiatives could serve as a mechanism to match policy commitments with available resources. They could also serve as a tool to monitor expenditure for the Commonwealth's gender management system (GMS), a holistic and system-wide approach to gender mainstreaming. Also, as budgets involve all government ministries and department, these initiatives could provide a practical opportunity for officials across sectors to integrate a gender analysis in their areas of work. Finally, given the central role of ministries of finance and planning in budget management and general governmental decision-making, GRB initiatives were seen as capable of introducing gender issues into the epicentre of government operations and financial management.

The 'How' of Gender-responsive Budgets

Gender-responsive budgets are inherently political. One dimension, which has been borne out in the Australian, South African and UK initiatives, is the association of gender with a specific political ideology or platform, rather than it being seen as an essential component of any development strategy. Another reality is that, while there are efficiency and equity arguments which justify the need for a gender analysis of government budgets, given the scarcity of resources and the competing demands that exist, politicians determine their strategic priorities based on their own understanding of the needs and preferences of their key constituencies. In the absence of gender-disaggregated data, the determination of gender needs or gaps can become largely arbitrary or be overlooked completely. A crucial factor, to the advancement of gender equality, therefore, is the effectiveness of the gender lobby.

The 1995 PoA was hugely significant in political terms within the Commonwealth Secretariat. Beyond the requirements for governments to take action, it mandated the Commonwealth Secretariat "to focus on and enhance its own experience and expertise in the critical areas of concern to play an effective coordinating role, provide leadership and assistance, and be an example of good practice" (Commonwealth Secretariat, 1995:16). It also required that the Secretariat send progress reports to the Commonwealth Heads of Government.

To ensure compliance in the Commonwealth Secretariat, a steering committee on gender and development, chaired by a deputy secretary-general and comprising all directors, was convened to monitor the performance of the organisation. All programmes were now required to implement gender projects. It was within this enabling environment that work on gender-responsive budgets took root. The economic programme divisions provided tentative support to the programme as a demonstration of their support for the organisational directive on gender mainstreaming. The Gender Section of the organisation was able to utilise this support in establishing the programme as an economic initiative in its own right.

By no stretch of the imagination did the commitments made under the PoA simply translate into the Commonwealth's GRB programme. The Commonwealth Secretariat had to confront the general belief in the Commonwealth and beyond, especially among most economists and finance officials, that gender was not a concern of, or relevant to, their work. Against this traditional wall of resistance, the Commonwealth Women's Ministers were of invaluable assistance.

At the 1996 Meeting of Commonwealth Ministers Responsible for Women's Affairs, the Ministers agreed that government budgets were the strategic entry point for engendering macroeconomic policies. Ministers called on Commonwealth countries to pilot this programme. They also undertook to work closely with their colleagues in finance to integrate a gender perspective into fiscal policy, and requested that the Commonwealth Secretariat develop tools and provide technical assistance to countries. This strategy seemed to pay early dividends as the 1996 Commonwealth Finance Ministers Meeting endorsed the Women's Ministers' recommendation to support an initial pilot programme.

Although the mandate from Women's Ministers was significant in mobilising support for country pilots within the Commonwealth, neither this nor an operational directive on gender mainstreaming could guarantee broad-based support in the Commonwealth Secretariat. The Gender Section had to develop a separate internal campaign to secure meaningful support from the economic programme divisions.

A key component of trying to generate commitment to the programme was the participation of prominent experts in the field who were able to supply the economists and finance officials with the economic justification, operational processes and expected results from implementing GRB initiatives. Diane Elson, a leading feminist economist, developed the conceptual framework for the integration of gender into macroeconomic policies (Elson, 1998: 41–52). Rhonda Sharp, one of the key 'femocrats' from the pioneering Women's Budget in Australia, and Debbie Budlender, a founding member of the South African Women's Budget Initiative, provided guidelines on how such a programme could be implemented.

The benefit of having champions for this cause in the organisation should not be overlooked. The evolution of the programme was driven in part by the passion of the then head of the Gender Section. It was further facilitated by the fact that senior managers in the organisation responded to the practicality of the programme. The support of two leading economists in the organisation, one of whom is now the head of the economic affairs programme and Secretary to the Finance Ministers' Meeting, also provided opportunities for the programme that many other gender and development initiatives have not benefited from.

What's Happening in GRB Initiatives?

The Commonwealth's international advocacy was largely successful. The Fifth Meeting of Commonwealth Ministers Responsible for Women's Affairs in 1996 was the first time that the issue of gender-responsive budgets was included on the agenda of an intergovernmental meeting. It will be discussed again as an agenda item of the 2002 Commonwealth Finance Ministers Meeting in September. This is the first time a meeting of finance ministers will discuss gender concerns as a specific agenda item. The Commonwealth Secretariat has also worked to raise awareness of the value of gender-responsive budgeting in different arenas, including at the United Nations and the Organisation of Economic Cooperation and

Development (OECD), and on a regional basis with the Asian Development Bank (ADB), Pacific Islands Forum and Southern African Development Community (SADC).

One of the strengths of the Commonwealth Secretariat's programme was to concentrate on one strategic area of fiscal policy. Government budgets contain two sides: expenditure and revenue. For reasons of both resource constraints and direct impact on the needs of women, the decision was taken to focus in the first instance on the expenditure side of the budget. The concentration of resources on a single, manageable area allowed for the development and refinement of the approach.

From the outset, one of the Commonwealth Secretariat's aims was to develop resources that could be utilised around the world in the implementation of GRB initiatives. These efforts culminated in the development of expenditure tools with different entry points for applying a gender analysis to government budgets (Elson, 2002: 44–47) and a methodology for implementing a country programme (Budlender & Sharp, 1998).

The Commonwealth Secretariat, in collaboration with its new programme partners, recently published Gender Budgets Makes Cents, an overview of the conceptual framework, methodology and outcomes at the country level. This book, Gender Budgets Makes More Cents, complements the earlier one by highlighting select country case studies and good practice. These publications on understanding GRB initiatives, which should be useful to a broad range of stakeholders, will be followed by a comprehensive reference manual and the development of a methodology for the analysis of the gender impacts of the revenue side of the budget.

The Commonwealth Secretariat's ability to encourage governments to implement GRB initiatives emerged as a result of the following organisational factors:

◆ The responsiveness of governments to its international advocacy;

◆ The access to ministers and senior officials of key ministries due to the organisation's nature and consensus-building mechanisms;

◆ The work of the technical assistance arm of the organisation which promotes gender mainstreaming as a cross-cutting theme of its development cooperation programme; and

◆ The effective networks between staff and government officials due to the size and purpose of the organisation. A related factor is the fact that many staff are seconded from their home civil services.

The initial success of the programme was also due to the strategy employed by the Commonwealth to introduce the initiative to governments. Requests for technical assistance from governments had to be submitted as a combined request of Finance and Women's Ministries. This requirement was a response to the realisation that, while Finance Ministries were best placed to coordinate implementation, their staff were often unable to make linkages between gender and economic issues. Similarly, Women's Ministries, while usually lacking knowledge of economics and budget processes, had the experience in gender mainstreaming and advocating for action within government on gender and development issues. This was often the first opportunity for these ministries to acquire an understanding of each other's portfolios and to work together. This was a significant outcome in itself.

The Australian and South African initiatives, and lessons learned, were used as the basis for the design of the methodology and training programme to build capacity at the country level. The value of these two country experiences, which were among the few known initiatives at the time, was not only their rarity but also their diversity. Having the participation of the two leading experts from Australia and South Africa involved in the capacity building also meant that these experiences were not used as a blue print but rather as guides, adapted to meet the situation of each country in terms of the prevailing gender issues, the resources available and the level of commitment.

The countries initially involved in the pilots were selected based on their diversity in terms of size, economic base and regional distribution. However common factors were also sought including the governments' commitment to gender and development and the capacity of the Finance and Women's Ministries.

Despite the care taken in the design and implementation of the programme, the Commonwealth country initiatives never attained sustainability. Governments were ambivalent about continuing with gender-responsive budgets without a clearly articulated demand. With finance officials largely unconcerned with gender issues and gender officials wary of getting into budget processes, external pressure in the form of advocacy, binding international agreements and development assistance was insufficient to maintain a commitment. The lesson learned was that civil society has a crucial role to play in this regard.

The Commonwealth Secretariat's primary function as an organisation providing assistance to its member governments was invaluable in terms of advocating to governments the need to adopt GRB initiatives. However, its primary function has been equally constraining in trying to access and involve non-government stakeholders in the implementation of the programme.

This constraint was overcome through the formation of the inter-agency partnership with the IDRC and UNIFEM. These new partners brought critical resources to the programme. UNIFEM works towards enhancing the role, capacity and participation of women, whereas IDRC focuses on building capacity in research, documentation and the sharing of experiences.

One of the most significant outcomes of the partnership has been the organisation of a high-level conference in October 2001 to share lessons learned and to mobilise political and financial support to meet the increasing demand from governments and civil society organisations to implement GRB initiatives. The conference was organised in collaboration with the Belgian government, the OECD and the Nordic Council of Ministers.

Conclusions

Gender-responsive budgets have been and should remain in the ownership of national stakeholders. Nonetheless, external agencies have a crucial support role to play. There are clear opportunities for them to engage in advocacy, produce resource materials, collaborate with stakeholders in the country on programme implementation, and support the adaptation of the programme to incorporate related development concerns including poverty reduction and civil society participation in decision-making.

Bibliography

Budlender D., D. Elson, G. Hewitt and T. Mukhopadhyay (2002). *Gender Budgets Makes Cents*. Commonwealth Secretariat, London.

Budlender D. and R. Sharp with K. Allen (1998). *How to do a gender-sensitive budget analysis: Contemporary research and practice*.

Commonwealth Secretariat/AusAID, London.

Commonwealth Secretariat (1998). *Gender Mainstreaming: Commonwealth Strategies on Politics, Macroeconomics and Human Rights.* Commonwealth Secretariat, London.

_____ (1997). *Report of the Fifth Meeting of Commonwealth Ministers Responsible for Women's Affairs.* Commonwealth Secretariat, London.

_____ (1995). *Commonwealth Plan of Action on Gender and Development.* Commonwealth Secretariat, London.

_____ (1992). *Commonwealth Notes: The Ottawa Declaration on Women and Structural Adjustment.* Commonwealth Secretariat, London.

_____ (1989). *Engendering Adjustment for the 1990s: Report of the Commonwealth Expert Group on Women and Structural Adjustment,* Commonwealth Secretariat, London.

Elson D. (2002). 'Integrating Gender into Government Budgets within a Context of Economic Reform' in D. Budlender, D. Elson, G. Hewitt & T. Mukhopadhyay *Gender Budgets Makes Cents,* Commonwealth Secretariat, London.

_____ (1998) 'Changing the Conceptual Framework to Integrate Gender into Macroeconomic Policies' in *Gender Mainstreaming: Commonwealth Strategies on Politics, Macroeconomics and Human Rights.* Commonwealth Secretariat, London.

Hewitt G. and T. Mukhopadhyay (2002). 'Promoting Gender Equality Through Public Expenditure' in D. Budlender, D. Elson, G. Hewitt and T. Mukhopadhyay *Gender Budgets Makes Cents.* Commonwealth Secretariat, London.

Inter-Parliamentary Union (2001). *Parliament and the Budgetary Process, Including from a Gender Perspective: Regional Seminar for English-Speaking Parliaments.* IPU, Geneva.

The Andean region: A multi-country programme

Rebecca Pearl[2]

[2] This chapter was written with input from Raquel Coello at UNIFEM-Andean Region and also draws on interviews with Magdalena Leon (Ecuador), Zonia Palán (Ecuador), Martha Gutierrez (Bolivia), and Bethsabé Andía (Peru).

Table 2: Selected Indicators for Bolivia, Ecuador and Peru

Indicator	Bolivia	Ecuador	Peru
Population	8.5 million	12.9 million	26.1 million
% of population which is female	51.7%	50.4%	51.3%
% of population which is urban	63%	62%	72%
Gross domestic product (gdp) per capita (US$)	2,355	2,944	4,622
Human development index (hdi)	0.648	0.726	0.743
Gender development index (gdi)	0.640	0.711	0.724
% of total budget funded by donors			
% of national parliamentarians who are women	10%	15%	18%

Source: Population Reference Bureau, 2001.

Introduction

The Andean region's experience with gender-responsive budget (GRB) initiatives is different from many others in its multi-country approach. Building on new attention toward women's economic and social rights in the region, and existing participatory budget initiatives throughout Latin America, the United Nations Development Fund for Women (UNIFEM) and local women's organisations launched a new round of GRB initiatives in Ecuador, Bolivia and Peru in March 2001.

From its regional office in Quito, Ecuador, UNIFEM-Andean Region facilitated six initiatives coordinated by small teams of researchers. The country teams and UNIFEM's programme coordinators based their work on the experiences of budget initiatives in Latin America and worldwide. They built on previous participatory and budget processes in the respective municipalities. The programme also built on a strong and vocal feminist movement in the Andean region.

While learning from other initiatives, UNIFEM developed a new methodology specific to the context and opportunities of the Andean Region countries. All the initiatives operated within the framework of a regional overarching programme to promote women's economic and social rights. The UNIFEM programme provided coordination, training and financial support, and monitored the results of the analysis. This multi-country approach allowed for one central coordinator to gather information, compare initiatives and facilitate cross-country learning.

In the first year the programme involved public forums on women's economic and social rights and capacity building on GRB initiatives This was followed by a first round of analysis by each of the teams. The programme will incorporate the lessons learned from firsthand experiences into the next round. The main lessons learned were:

◆ these initiatives should always begin with a review of gender inequities and women's needs;

◆ the political climate should be open to policy and budget inputs from outside the government administration;

◆ civil servants who have agreed to participate in the initiative should receive training, especially on gender, and be involved in the initiative from the beginning in order to facilitate access to information and decision-making processes; and

◆ civil society partners, who have important monitoring and advocacy roles, should also be involved from the beginning.

This chapter reviews the steps taken by UNIFEM in the Andean Region to strengthen the public climate for GRB initiatives. It examines the experiences of four initiatives in the region and highlights lessons that can be applied to other initiatives.

Context and Methodology

UNIFEM coordinates GRB initiatives in the Andean Region as part of its Programme on Women's Economic and Social Rights. This programme was launched in 2000 as a three-year campaign in Bolivia, Colombia, Ecuador and Peru. The programme's main strategies are to integrate women's economic and social rights established in international legislation into public policy, to create public consciousness about these rights through training workshops, to facilitate GRB analysis and advocacy and to make economic and social rights more visible through various means of communication.

The first year of the programme laid the groundwork for promoting economic and social rights in the region. UNIFEM held an international expert meeting to consult with its partners in the women's movement, economists, government and civil society. Given the devastating poverty and gender inequities enveloping Latin America, and with the human rights discourse in the region now including an understanding of economic, social and cultural rights, there was a call for practical tools to improve women's rights, broaden the public's understanding of human rights and make a strong link to the daily reality of Andean women. The new GRB programme took place in the context of a growing number of mechanisms for citizen participation, municipal accountability and transparency in the region.

UNIFEM's work on GRB initiatives began in October 2000, although the analysis did not begin until a year later. The first year focused on creating awareness and understanding of GRB initiatives in Latin America and elsewhere. The Latin American experience was documented in the research paper, "Gender Sensitive Budgets: Experiences in Latin America" (Vargas, 2000). The research focused on budget initiatives in Brazil and Ecuador, and initiatives that included a gender perspective in Chile, Mexico and Peru. This document, and extensive research conducted on economic and social rights and on GRB work, served as a knowledge base for the programme.

In October 2000 UNIFEM and Ecuador's National Council of Women (CONAMU) organised a public panel on National Budgets for Equity. This served as the formal launch of the Programme on Economic and Social Rights. The title of this panel, excluding words such as 'gender' and 'women', was intentional as there is a strong climate throughout Latin America opposing consideration of gender or women's concerns. Even United Nations officials, during a training session organised by the UN Working Group on Gender in Ecuador, admitted that they were not likely to attend events that addressed gender. About 200 people, representing many of UNIFEM's partners, government and United Nations officials, as well as groups of indigenous women and women working in the informal sector, attended the panel. UNIFEM also publicised the new programme at a parallel event, the World

Bank/Inter-American Development Bank Latin America Gender and Development Seminar.

To launch the new series of GRB initiatives in the Andean Region, UNIFEM then organised a Latin American Workshop on Participatory Gender Sensitive Budgets in Quito in March 2001. The training was targeted to two types of participants: players in Andean Region countries already involved in budget initiatives and willing to consider integrating a gender focus; and those countries within the hemisphere that, based on their own experiences, could provide advocacy or practical support. The thirty participants from civil society and women's organisations, women's ministries, budget offices and international development banks came from Barbados, Bolivia, Brazil, Chile, Colombia, Ecuador, Mexico, Peru, Uruguay and the United States. Two to three participants from each of the main target countries worked in small groups in order to facilitate concrete follow-up activities in Bolivia, Colombia, Ecuador and Peru. Individuals representing the other countries brought a perspective from outside the Andean Region to the small working groups.

The programme drew on methodologies from other GRB initiatives and built on existing participatory budget processes in municipalities. It was important for those in the Andean Region to learn what could be replicated or adapted to their specific contexts. The training introduced the experiences of South Africa, Mexico and other countries to demonstrate the best conditions for these initiatives. Two public panels allowed the group to learn from municipalities in Brazil, Chile and Ecuador as well.

Latin America's approach to budget transparency has often involved a participatory methodology, exemplified by community consultations undertaken by the municipality of Porto Alegre in Brazil. During the training, the group considered new laws governing citizen participation. Participants who were less familiar with gender analysis learned how women's participation is fundamental to ensuring government accountability. The group separated by country into small working groups which were encouraged to consider tools used in other initiatives, but also to develop new methodology appropriate to their countries.

Four Initiatives in the Andean Region

Six teams participated in this multi-country programme. Four were in Ecuador and one each was in Peru and Bolivia. The initiatives in Ecuador were launched in the capital municipality of Quito, jointly in Quito's Central Zone and rural Salitre, in Cuenca, and jointly in Esmeraldas, Colta, and Chambo. In Peru an initiative was launched in the district of Villa El Salvador in the capital city, Lima. In Bolivia an initiative looked at the national budget and the capital municipality of La Paz.

Each country team took a different approach, due to the different political opportunities in each country and the expertise and personal preferences of the participants. Some teams sought to apply the methodology of the training workshop while others adapted it. This resulted in diverse approaches and a range of lessons learned. In most cases these initiatives were the first attempts at GRB analysis in the municipalities, but most participants had experience with budget analysis and promoting citizen participation in municipal decision-making.

At the outset of the programme, UNIFEM identified the ideal components for these initiatives in the Andean region. These included an initial analysis of the situation of women and gender equity conditions, a political climate open to reform and public participation, training of civil servants, dissemination of the analysis results to government and civil society, and arrangements for civil society follow-up. By the end of the first round of analysis, the extent of the programme's adherence to these components reflected the first attempt at bringing this tool to the region. There were thus both successes and room for improvement. Two out of six initiatives looked at women's conditions before launching the analysis. Four initiatives were working in a favourable political climate. None of the initiatives succeeded in a thorough training of civil servants. Five initiatives disseminated their results to the government and civil society and five initiatives arranged for civil society follow-up.

The advantage of connecting these initiatives in a multi-country programme was a high learning curve. By coordinating six teams with diverse experiences, UNIFEM could determine which analytical tools were effective in specific municipalities and why certain methods worked better than others in each context.

27

Bolivia: National budget and La Paz

A team of two researchers looked at Bolivia's national budget and the budget of the municipality of the nation's capital, La Paz. Bolivia is the poorest country in the Andean Region, with indicators that are similar to those of some African countries. The country's new Popular Participation Law mandates citizen involvement in policy decisions. This provided an important institutional entry point for the work.

The Bolivian initiative adapted the methodology presented in the training and developed a new approach to gender-responsive budgets based on 'budget constraints'. They found that budget items such as debt repayment received the bulk of government spending and therefore limited the possibility of investing more in social concerns. The analysis showed that redistribution of funds in a gender responsive way was blocked by the prevailing institutional framework. The principal researcher's personal contacts and extensive knowledge of budget processes allowed her to navigate the municipality of La Paz and national departments and find the necessary data.

The methodology used in Bolivia set out to build a public culture of understanding around the municipal development plan and the annual operative programme. It focused, in particular, on the spending destined to take forward the Bolivian Poverty Reduction Strategy Paper (PRSP). In Bolivia, women and other civil society groups participate in budget formation as part of the decentralisation reform outlined in the Popular Participation Law. However, women are often not involved in budget implementation and monitoring. The Bolivian initiative also seeks to empower women and women's organisations to influence budget decisions and do advocacy work with municipal and national governments by building women's technical budget expertise.

The initiative first looked at budget constraints, so as to identify the financial commitments of the municipality that restricted spending on alternative categories. The level of budget inflexibility was determined to be 71 per cent for 1999, implying that a maximum of 29 per cent of the budget could be reassigned to gender-responsive goals. In the analysis, the initiative did not consider the possible differential impact of the restricted 71 per cent of the budget on women and men.

In analysing the impact of government spending, the principal researcher drew on methodology from the international training. She examined 2,500 projects that are part of the municipal public investment programme and found that scarcely 3 per cent of this programme was dedicated to projects with direct impact on women's needs, and that there were no projects focused on men. The programme made no investment in increasing equal opportunity in public sector employment, but 97 per cent of the programme had the capacity to generate indirect impacts for the specific demands of women.

The Bolivian initiative uncovered an important gap in participatory budget planning. While public involvement in budget decisions is mandated through the Popular Participation Law, less than half of the spending determined by participatory planning had been applied. Technical capacity and institutional management are possible causes. The Popular Participation Law transfers resources to the administration of basic health and education services, but this does not provide for a complete restructuring that would free up new resources.

Gender equity is mentioned in the five-year municipal development plan of La Paz due to women's participation in the planning process. However, the analysis revealed that the budget was largely devoted to urban development planning, which the municipality does not consider to have gendered impacts. Spending decisions often lagged behind policy decisions, especially in terms of incorporating gender and social equity.

One of UNIFEM's biggest challenges has been finding people in Latin America who have experience with both gender and economics. In Bolivia, the team consisted of two people. An expert in public finance, who had years of experience with the government and knowledge of its inner workings, served as the principal researcher. She knew how to access data and was familiar with how the municipality and national government worked from the inside. The data she found on a public website was not disaggregated by gender, but she used a government database on municipal projects, which detailed spending and beneficiaries, to separate the numbers between women and men. A second researcher with a background in gender analysis contributed the gender component to the team. The two researchers conducted their work separately. In retrospect, the initiative would have benefited from a joint approach combining the researchers' municipal and gender expertise.

Another critical lesson learned in this initiative was the importance of including civil society organisations early on in the process. The

Bolivian Women's Coordinating Organisation planned events to present the results of the analysis to the public, but civil society groups were not involved in the analysis itself. A future phase of the programme will probably focus on the municipality of Cochabamba, where women's organisations will participate in the training and be more involved in subsequent advocacy work.

The initial results of the analysis were presented in public meetings in the capital, and were attended by national and municipal civil society groups, international donor agencies and budget officials. On International Women's Day, the results were published in a city newspaper. In response to this, the Vice Minister for Gender Concerns showed interest in a short-term action programme on gender. However, the initiative as a whole did not build on any initial demand within the Bolivian federal government or within the municipality. It was the principal researcher's own resourcefulness that made the data collection a success, and the government did not express interest in conducting a budget analysis.

This first project was intended to serve as a model for replication in other Bolivian municipalities. There is still work needed to conduct a comprehensive gender analysis, and determine how to apply a gender lens to budget sections not usually associated with gender. The second researcher in Bolivia, with expertise in gender and municipal management, suggests a more in-depth study of constitutional matters, like decentralisation, in future phases of the initiative. Also, a better definition of indicators would allow a more accurate measure of the impact of policies and budgets on women's lives. Further challenges are to use a more rigorous gender analysis, and to establish more lasting entry points in the government and commitment from civil society to ensure implementation of the analysis.

Ecuador: Quito and Salitre

The recent economic and debt crises in Latin America, and the adoption of the United States dollar as the official currency, have further decreased the standard of living of many people in Ecuador, especially women. Ecuador's national government has taken some limited steps to promote gender equity. Article 41 of Ecuador's constitution calls on the state to "formulate and execute policies that promote equal opportunities for men and women…and incorporate a gender perspective in the state's plans and programmes." A quota law of 1998 requires 30 per cent representation of women on ballots at all levels, from national to local. During the first local election to apply this law in May 2000, almost 25 per cent of 3,870 newly elected representatives were women. More women than before have entered the paid workforce in Ecuador, but wage inequalities have worsened and discrimination has pushed women into the informal sector.

One of the initiatives launched in Ecuador focused on the budget of the capital municipality, Quito. A second initiative looked at the municipality of Salitre, a rural town on the coast of Ecuador. Other initiatives in the country had less information available at the time of writing.

Quito

The municipality of Quito's initiative was coordinated by an economist and two assistants from the Women's Political Coordinating Organisation, a national civil society organisation with strong ties to women politicians. It built on the organisation's previous analysis of the municipality's budget process.

The initiative looked at the 2002 budget to determine how the Mayor's development plan, Quito's 21st Century Plan, translated into funding and whether the gender elements from the plan were included in the budget. Although the Mayor's political campaign was based on this development plan, which calls for gender equity in development projects, gender was not mainstreamed through the plan and a gender perspective was still not considered relevant to public works and international policies. Further, the Mayor's plan is not yet institutionalised and is often forgotten for months at a time, occasionally surfacing when it becomes relevant. The municipality's Commission on Women, Children and Family, collaborating with the community women's council, developed a plan called Building Gender Equity. Since the project did not have its own funding, however, the demands it outlined could only be addressed indirectly in the municipality's projects, rather than mainstreamed throughout the administration.

Like the Mayor's plan, the budget lacked an overall integration of gender, so the team identified a number of projects which mentioned gender explicitly. However, even decisions made by the municipality to include gender projects in the 2002 budget were not reflected effectively. For example, the budget failed to designate 15 per cent of the municipal budget to the Fund for Equity and Solidarity Between Men and Women, as agreed to by municipal equity committees.

The researchers found that the budget in Quito is largely defined by individual departments. For example, the social department develops projects for women related to health or domestic violence. As a result of this, women-directed policies were compartmentalised into one department and women were not considered direct beneficiaries in projects related to infrastructure, housing and a range of other issues.

Only one of the eight zones comprising the municipality incorporated gender explicitly. In the project planning of the other seven zones, beneficiaries of projects were identified as 'all residents' with no distinction made between women and men. The initiative made a recommendation for each of these projects to include 30 per cent women in the list of beneficiaries, following the country's new quota law.

The majority of Quito's 8,000 municipal workers are men. In all eight municipal zones, gender inequity was prevalent in the municipality's salary and position levels. The initiative recommended gender balance in hiring and that 30 per cent of contracting jobs for public works be assigned to women. It noted that in education, male teachers generally receive a higher salary than women, even though there are many more women teachers. Schools often have a male principal with all female teachers.

The initiative looked briefly at government income, although there were no statistics available on taxation. It was difficult to gauge women's contribution to government income because their roles are not formalised through property or business ownership. As the majority of women are not property owners and many are engaged in informal work, which is not taxed, they provide less income to the state through taxes. It was noted however that women often made payments even though the property was not in their name. Further, there was a need to determine how many women were involved in the informal economy. It would also be interesting to determine whether income received by the municipality is reinvested in a gender-insensitive way because women's contribution to tax is comparatively small. As much gender-disaggregated data does not exist, the initiative requested the government to incorporate gender into the property registry system.

The initiative is currently trying to determine whether the

municipality's new budget formulation process is a positive reform for women. The previous process simply increased the budget by the inflation rate. Under the new law, each department and all eight zone administrations create their own programming to be approved individually by the municipality. The sum of all projects and administrative costs add up to the overall budget amount. While the municipality does not currently operate a participatory budget process, there are plans to do so in 2003, starting with some of the smaller zone administrations.

UNIFEM has had an important role in demystifying the budget for women's organisations in Quito. Budget analysis and advocacy is usually reserved for economists. These initiatives brought women closer to the budget and opened a dialogue on women's role in financial management, both at the municipal and household levels. Learning how other initiatives were being implemented in Peru, Mexico and Chile was useful for the Quito initiative. Comparing experiences helped in developing a methodology specific to the region and locality. UNIFEM also introduced the idea of creating vigilance groups of women to monitor the budget.

The women's movement in Quito benefited from the support of a councilwoman who is a strong women's advocate. Although this was an important entry point in the municipality and there was significant political will from the Mayor of Quito, there was limited institutional capacity to carry out this commitment. Securing information was easier for this initiative than for other teams in Ecuador, but the initiative would have benefited from a contact person inside the municipality who had the capacity and time to navigate the system better.

Salitre

The Latin American Network of Women Transforming the Economy, which also conducted an analysis in Quito's central zone, coordinated the Salitre initiative. The main challenges in Salitre were gaining and maintaining entry points in the municipality, accessing data, training women to understand the budget and work with the municipal administration, and helping them to envision their demands.

The initiative set minimal requirements for beginning work which were similar to other teams. The municipality had to show political commitment to citizen participation and gender mainstreaming, there

33

had to be a connection with women in the municipality, and the municipality had to facilitate access to information. The team also stipulated that women's organisations had to accompany the process, sensitising the community to gender budgets and monitoring the results. It identified an important connection with the Mayor and, equally significant, his wife, and with local women's organisations.

During an initial workshop women received training on understanding the budget, and were asked to think about their community and work roles, and to set out their needs and criteria for redistributing resources. The analysis looked at the distribution of government spending and income, how funds are spent, what channels allow women to access this information, and what internal bureaucratic mechanisms distance the women from the budget. A final workshop was proposed to present the results of the analysis and plan for follow-up and monitoring.

The experience of citizen participation in the small rural town of Salitre is different from that seen in its sister initiative in Quito's central zone. Gender discrimination is more prevalent in rural areas and on the coast of Ecuador. Participation is part of the political discourse in Salitre, but not institutionalised. In contrast, Quito's central zone is a large urban administration that has experience interacting with community-based groups, although an official participatory budget process is not yet in place. The Mayor's office in Quito has developed people's councils with youth, the elderly and women, and women's demands have been incorporated into the municipal plan.

There were few channels for women to participate in decision-making in Salitre. Women had little experience interacting with the municipality and limited knowledge of its institutional structure. Women's organisations in the past focused on rural issues, like the demands of agricultural workers, and issues related to survival and motherhood, like education and health. Women from Salitre met with women from the coastal city of Guayaquil, a group that struggles with floods and a crisis in rice production. The exchange between these two groups of women pushed the Salitre group to approach the municipality as a people's council for the first time, present their demands, and sign an agreement with the Mayor.

The initiative made an initial step toward opening the municipality to themes that officials had not considered part of their responsibility.

Women wanted the municipality to address the high rates of domestic violence in Salitre, and demanded a department for reporting these incidents under anti-violence laws. The municipality responded that this demand would have to be addressed through other levels of government, but the women did win a designated space for their meetings in the municipal building. This is a symbolic space for women where university law students intern to defend women's legal rights in the community. Winning the meeting space was also an immediate gain that opened up a dialogue with the municipality.

In Salitre, getting access to data and the budget was a difficult task. There seemed to be little clarity about the final budget and how funds were distributed within the municipality itself. There was also some level of unwillingness to expose budget decisions to the community. The women had to approach the municipality carefully and convince civil servants that the community's access to information would not threaten the municipality or the Mayor. When the women formed their council, there was no information about the current year's budget. They only knew that a small amount of money in the previous year's budget responded to the demands they had presented. This token amount was considered a step toward municipal accountability to women's organisations rather than significant funding. Access to budget and municipal information was also difficult in Quito's central zone, forcing the team to spend much time pressuring multiple offices to release different pieces of data.

Another difficulty shared by Salitre and Quito's central zone was how women define their demands and needs. Community women's groups were not accustomed to looking at budgets. Interaction between the municipality of Salitre and the community normally focused on improving the community's infrastructure, like roads and sidewalks. Public works were seen as tangible progress, while childcare and health funding were less visible investments. Women had a difficult time seeing themselves in the role of analysing the budget and making demands of the municipality. They were concerned that redistributing funds might detract from other important issues, and were not accustomed to valuing their own needs as a priority of the government.

Salitre faced the common challenge of finding coordinators familiar with both gender and budgets. An economist who worked in Ecuador's central bank attended the international training, but had little knowledge of gender and the women's movement. The initiative thus chose to work with a different researcher, an economist from Guayaquil who had worked for a long time with women in the social sector. Although she had not participated in UNIFEM's international training, she was comfortable with helping the women understand the gender budgets methodology due to her knowledge of both gender and economics. In addition, Salitre benefited from learning about work done in Guayaquil, Ecuador's most populous city and also on the coast.

Another challenge was that participants found that undertaking a GRB initiative required sustained and long-term development of women's participation. In rural Salitre, it was difficult to mobilise women's involvement because time spent on meetings and other activities took them away from their work obligations in the household and community. Each day of activities required transportation, long trips to and from the outer communities, arranging for childcare and other logistical obstacles.

In a meeting with the initiative coordinators in Salitre, the municipal councillors, all men, committed themselves to working on gender equity. However, despite the signed agreement it made with the women's group, there is little certainty that the municipality will adopt the results of the analysis. These results and the new women's meeting space are nevertheless very important first steps toward municipal accountability for the women's organisations. Gender is still a marginalised theme in Salitre and changing the municipality's attitude will depend on sustained pressure from the women's organisations.

The entry point for GRB analysis in Salitre was more informal than that of urban initiatives. Although there were no councilwomen in Salitre, the Mayor's wife agreed to assist the initiative and played an important role forming a bridge between councillors and the community. She sponsors community works and special events with the wives of other councillors. This group of women has little experience in municipal management, but is committed to advancing the causes of the women's movement.

The initiative coordinator learned from the experience of Porto Alegre, Brazil, where there is a rich history of public participation. Based on Porto Alegre's and Salitre's experiences, she concluded that in order to implement gender-responsive budgets, you need first to ensure a process of citizen participation. The Salitre team also found a similarity in the way that community demands for education and health are not considered as municipal responsibilities. In both initiatives, municipal law did not mandate a provision of these social services, but they were won in Porto Alegre and initially discussed in Salitre via public pressure. The experiences of Porto Alegre and other budget initiatives have taught the Salitre team that facilitating a community's understanding of women's work roles will not happen overnight. Opening an environment of participation, political will and sensitivity to gender issues is essential, and may take an extended period of time.

Peru: Villa El Salvador

The initiative in Villa El Salvador was led by a team of two researchers: a university professor with expertise in budget analysis and a gender expert. Villa El Salvador is a district of Peru's capital that is well-known in Latin America for participatory development planning. The team worked diligently to follow the methodology presented in the international training and developed new ways to analyse the available information when necessary. Women's civil society organisations were invited into the process from the beginning. The municipality was also involved from the outset and signed an agreement with UNIFEM to launch the analysis.

The gender budget initiative in Peru was launched at the close of an era of political turmoil. The initial strategy session with regional practitioners was held in Lima a few days after Alberto Fujimori stepped down from the presidency. The participation of an official from Peru's finance ministry in this session suggested that the political shift would offer new entry points for GRB analysis. Peru has a higher standard of living than Bolivia and Ecuador and also benefits from a strong women's movement.

Villa El Salvador's rich history of public participation in municipal development is highlighted by the motto of the district's first development plan, "Because we have nothing we will do everything." Villa El Salvador's entire population of 340,000 inhabitants once fell within the poorest economic bracket of the capital, according to official statistics. The district's ten-year development plan grew out of consultations with about 50,000 people and was approved in a vote by 93 per cent of the district's population. Learning from the participatory budget experiences of Porto Alegre and San André in Brazil, Guyana in Venezuela and Montevideo in Uruguay, the municipality formed a district assembly to transform the development plan into a participatory budget. A substantial sum from the municipality was distributed to the various zones, and 100 per cent of this budget was executed as set out in the plan. Villa El Salvador's participatory budget process created a community experienced in participation and community mobilisation, and a transparent municipal budget with 30 per cent reinvestment in the municipality. It has inspired replication of this process in other municipalities in Peru.

The international training convinced the Peruvian team to undertake an analysis of Villa El Salvador's ten-year development plan from a gender perspective. The team set out to follow the methodology of the South African initiative very closely, but later found it necessary to develop new tools more appropriate for the Peruvian context. The team first looked at gender in municipal policy. They conducted research on the subject, and reviewed studies by civil society organisations on how women in Villa El Salvador perceived their needs. The team reviewed whether resources assigned to policies would change gender inequalities, by comparing the development plan to the budget and information from Villa El Salvador's gender roundtable.

The second step in their analysis evaluated spending in the categories set out by the international training, including specific spending on women, spending on gender equity in employment and general spending on community access to services. The team found that resources targeted directly to women were non-existent and the municipal budget did not address which groups in the community, for instance women or men, would have access to services.

The Peruvian team evaluated the inclusion of gender in all municipal projects and programmes, including departments focused on youth, community services, human development, urban development, economic development and administration. For each of these departments the team conducted interviews to understand the role of women, women's access to departmental resources, and in what way those resources improved women's situation.

The municipality does not collect information on the beneficiaries of services and how funds are spent. This made it virtually impossible to evaluate the differences between men and women. Even aggregated data was difficult to secure. However, the team managed to disaggregate some information by gender and compare the numbers to the municipality's total spending. When the information was completely insufficient, the team turned to qualitative analysis, arranging interviews with beneficiaries of services.

An important contribution of this team was how they looked at the proportion of women's work and time use in municipal services. Villa El Salvador is a municipality with many so-called 'self-managing' services. Under this approach, a community health centre may have doctors working half of their time on a volunteer basis. The government may supply basic materials and food to soup kitchens while women in the community provide the labour. The initiative measured what proportion of municipal services were supported by women's work, and how much of women's time was invested in the functioning of these services. For example, the time use study was applied to the Glass of Milk Programme, a food assistance programme that takes up one third of the municipal budget and is supported by three million US dollars annually. The team determined that women's unpaid work was equal to 20 per cent of the total budget of the Glass of Milk Programme.

The initiative struggled to find lasting commitment to gender in this small municipality. The budget director attended the international training and assisted with access to information, but municipal officials did not attend presentations on the team's findings and there was little clarity about how the analysis would impact policy, despite the signed agreement with UNIFEM.

Although the municipality was not responsive to gender there is a strong and organised women's movement, led by the Women's Popular Federation (FEPOMUVES), which has experience collaborating with Villa El Salvador's gender roundtable. Women from this organisation were trained in budget analysis, formed a committee to monitor implementation of the analysis and will be involved in advocacy work.

UNIFEM considers the Peruvian initiative, with its creativity in developing the methodology and ability to assess gender and budget processes jointly, as one of the most successful initiatives. In the future, the team will need to strengthen entry points within the municipality.

Lessons Learned

A significant challenge in this programme was bringing together all of the essential elements into each initiative, especially political will, civil society engagement, and professional expertise in both gender and budgets. With limited data available and accessible in the municipalities, teams needed to go beyond an analysis of spending categories and strengthen the methodology of qualitative analysis. New training might look at how to navigate municipal systems and access information, and at more creative ways of translating limited data into gender indicators.

This was UNIFEM-Andean Region's first experience facilitating this kind of programme, so it was a process of constant learning for everyone involved. Unexpected obstacles or changes require a certain level of flexibility when implementing a new and large multi-country programme. In a few cases, key government officials who agreed to collaborate with an initiative did not follow through. The time it took to come to agreements with initiative partners was longer than expected, which delayed the presentation of results and first follow-up meeting. UNIFEM's funding and decision-making is tied to the larger bureaucracy of the United Nations, which created obstacles that are different from an initiative that emerges from a community-based organisation.

From the perspective of the teams, one of the biggest contributions of the programme is bringing the new concept of gender-responsive budgets to the region in the first place. In some cases, existing budget initiatives were re-launched to integrate a gender perspective. Since UNIFEM is not directly involved in on-the-ground implementation, it served as a facilitating partner. It sought to be a focal point for networking all of the initiatives both to each other and to international initiatives outside the Andean region. Teams had the opportunity to exchange experiences in trainings and follow-up meetings. UNIFEM's role was to guide the development of methodology that responds to the needs of women and the Andean Region context. The programme facilitated follow-up and advocacy mechanisms and used existing and new political connections to help identify entry points for the analysis.

While some of the participants in the international training followed the presented methodology to the letter, others came up against difficulties and worked to reorient the methodology. Except for the team in Peru, most researchers in the programme were frustrated by the lack of data available through their municipalities and instead concentrated on the identification of spending categories. UNIFEM-Andean Region viewed Bolivia's focus on budget constraints as a realistic approach, given the lack of flexibility in the prevailing budget structure. Some participants stumbled when trying to extract qualitative information from the budget, like the impact of women's time use in Peru. They found that this analysis requires more gender-disaggregated and qualitative information, such as assessing the quality of services through focal groups with the community. This requires an enormous amount of research, and the teams did not have the capacity to do it themselves.

UNIFEM's first obstacle was identifying people with enough experience to coordinate the initiatives. Participants in the programme had varying opinions about whether it is easier for a public finance expert or a gender expert to undertake GRB initiatives. It may be difficult for a traditionally trained economist to integrate a gender perspective into their thinking, but it may also be difficult for someone from the women's movement to understand budgets, navigate municipalities and have the right political connections. There are very few people with experience in both fields, and the best solution has been a team of coordinators with complementary expertise.

Working at the municipal level had advantages over the national level in Latin America. Many countries were already going through decentralisation reform and instituting participatory mechanisms at the local level to enhance accountability and transparency. While the programme encouraged existing national level budget initiatives to include a stronger gender perspective, UNIFEM did not have the capacity or resources to work at that level. An advantage of coordinating this programme from a UN agency was the heightened international visibility and interest that the GRB analysis received, and the possibility of replicating a practical tool for gender analysis to other municipalities in the region and beyond.

In a Mini-Strategic Planning Workshop with UNIFEM officials based in Latin America, UNIFEM-Andean Region shared its experience in coordinating this multi-country GRB programme. The lessons shared reinforced the methodology of the initial training and echoed what other practitioners have found in other countries and regions. UNIFEM's requirements to complete a gender-sensitive budget analysis are:

◆ A diagnosis where women's needs and interests are identified and defined;

◆ Political will;

◆ Civil servants trained and sensitised;

◆ Analysis that focuses on the previous year's budget and makes recommendations for the upcoming budget;

◆ Dissemination of recommendations and results to government and civil society and

◆ Civil society follow-up, for example, in the form of vigilance committees (Coello, 2002).

UNIFEM-Andean Region's GRB programme is only in its initial stages. The methodology will continue to evolve to strengthen women's rights and improve gender equity in the region. At the 2001 World Social Forum in Porto Alegre, Brazil, UNIFEM-Andean Region organised a panel on gender-responsive budgets. The enormous enthusiasm of the participants expanded the programme from the Andean Region to the level of Latin America.

References

Coello R. (2002). "Gender-Sensitive Budgets: The Andean Region Experience." Presentation for UNIFEM Mini-Strategic Planning Workshop, Quito.

Vargas V. (2000). "Gender Sensitive Budgets: Experiences in Latin America." Paper presented at the Sixth International Course on Women's Human Rights: Economic and Social Rights, organized by Manuela Ramos, Lima.

Australia: The mandarin approach to gender budgets

Marian Sawer

Table 3: Selected Indicators for Australia

Indicator	*Year*	*Number*
Population	2001	19.4m
% of population which is female	2001	50.2
% of population which is urban	1996	86
Gross domestic product (GDP) per capita (US$)	1999	28,433
Human development index (HDI)	1999	0.936
Gender development index (GDI)	1999	0.935
% of total budget funded by donors	2002	0
% of national parliamentarians who are women	2001	25.3

Introduction

Australia has a federal political system comprising six State governments, two Territory governments, and the Commonwealth (or Federal) government[3]. This paper describes Australia's experience of gender budgeting at the Federal level, where it was introduced in 1984. It will also highlight experiences at the sub-national level, as State and Territory governments followed the Federal lead.

In 1972 a new Federal government was elected in Australia, with an election commitment to make government more responsive to women. The feminists recruited for this purpose – who became known as 'femocrats' – developed a model of women's policy machinery that emphasised the importance of mainstreaming gender analysis into central policy processes. From the beginning they had a clear perception that mainstream policies, such as tariffs, industry policy and industrial relations, had more impact on women's lives than the

[3] In order to avoid confusion, the Commonwealth government of Australia will be referred to as the Federal government where possible.

relatively small programme expenditures on women's or children's services or equity programmes in education and employment. This is not to under-rate the significance of the innovative approach to delivery of women's services and to the development of national policies that the presence of femocrats made possible. However, it was their focus on policy monitoring and policy audit that was most distinctive.

By the mid-1970s the hub of Australian women's policy machinery was situated in the chief policy coordinating arm of the Federal government, the Department of Prime Minister and Cabinet. What became the Office of the Status of Women (OSW) had responsibility for analysis of all Cabinet submissions for gender impact, regardless of the area of government from which they came. Decentralised units of this machinery were established in line departments of government. These were intended to detect and report on gender impact before proposals had reached the stage of a Cabinet submission.

In line with their commitment to mainstreaming, Australian femocrats became increasingly concerned with the need for an effective way to mainstream gender perspectives and gender accountability into budgetary processes. This led to the invention of the women's budget process – most commonly known in Australia as the 'women's budget statement' – which was facilitated by the key location of the OSW. The statement was intended to require government agencies to audit all their activity for its impact on women, not just programmes specifically directed to women. The terms gender budgeting or gender-sensitive budgeting have more recently been used internationally to describe much the same process.

Women's budgeting at the Federal level, and to varying degrees at other levels of government in Australia, played an important role in raising awareness that apparently gender-neutral programmes are not necessarily gender-neutral in impact. Further, this is true of economic as well as social portfolios. Over time, however, the original purpose of the women's budget process became eroded and it became a form of public relations rather than an analytic tool. While it was originally intended to highlight the differential impact on women of 'mainstream' budgetary allocations, as well as to highlight expenditures targeted to women, the latter function had become dominant by the time of its demise. This is one of the dangers of a bureaucratic strategy.

History of the Federal Women's Budget

The women's budget programme was first introduced in time for the 1984 Federal budget. It arose out of discussion at one of the regular meetings of Federal, State and Territory 'women's advisers' (a generic term for the senior feminist policy bureaucrat in each jurisdiction). At first this was generally the head of a policy unit in a Premier's or Prime Minister's Department, but more recently in New South Wales it was the head of the Department for Women. These quarterly meetings were conducted on a frank and informal basis and were a useful forum for pooling ideas and experience and for policy learning, particularly on the part of newly appointed advisers.

On this occasion discussion was initiated by one of the State women's advisers on how to exercise some leverage on 'mainstream' budget expenditures, which were far more important in terms of effect on the social and economic status of women than the relatively small programmes dedicated to improving the position of women. The idea was taken away from this meeting and developed by Anne Summers, newly appointed head of OSW in the Department of Prime Minister and Cabinet. Dr Summers had a background as a founder of Australia's first women's shelter in 1974, as the author of a best-selling feminist history of Australia, as a founder of a successful feminist journal, as a senior political journalist and associate editor of the *Australian Financial Review*, and as president of the Federal parliamentary press gallery.

Cabinet approval for this radical initiative was achieved through the Secretaries' Taskforce on the Status of Women. This was a high-level coordinating mechanism established as a result of a 1983 election commitment and made up of departmental heads. The Labor Party's women's policy had been drafted by a former femocrat, who perceived that inter-departmental coordination on the status of women needed to be conducted at a more senior level to be effective. However, the new body, chaired by the head of the Prime Minister's Department, the most senior bureaucrat in the government, had not yet been given anything to do. Establishment of a cross-portfolio women's budget process was an ideal agenda item. The existence of 'slack resources' was thus an important contribution to policy innovation.

As a consequence of endorsement at this level, Cabinet approved the introduction of a process whereby Federal departments and agencies were required to provide a detailed account of the impact of their activities on women, to be included in a document circulated by the Prime Minister on budget night. This process greatly enhanced the effectiveness of the token requirement introduced in the 1983 Cabinet Handbook that all Cabinet submissions include a statement indicating their impact on women. In addition to analysis of the impact of existing programmes and policies, departments were expected to identify objectives and mechanisms to improve performance in meeting the needs of women.

The women's budget programme was introduced on a trial basis in about half the government departments in 1984. It was introduced on a full-scale basis covering all departments and portfolio agencies from 1985. A useful feature of the first women's budget, which was later replicated at the State level, was a list of government commitments to women made in the very detailed election policy and an account of progress made in implementing them.

As Cabinet approval had only been received a few weeks before the budget was due to be tabled, the women's budget was produced very quickly. One hiccough was the discovery, on the morning of the budget, that part of a confidential report on a candidate for promotion had mysteriously appeared in place of a footnote in the Social Security contribution. Large numbers of public servants in the Department of Prime Minister and Cabinet had to be employed sticking labels over the offending passage in all the copies so that the women's budget programme could be duly tabled in parliament in the evening.

From 1987 the women's budget programme was renamed the women's budget statement and given more formal status. Once the women's budget covered all Federal government activity it became a very substantial document, averaging about 300 pages until 1994. To make up for the intimidating character of a document aiming to extract detailed accountability from departments, the print run of the full document was reduced from 6,000 to 1,000 copies from 1987. A shorter, illustrated version of 32 pages was published for the use of women's groups.

The women's budget played an important role, particularly in its early years, in educating bureaucrats and sensitising departments to the impact of their policies on women in the community. Public servants had traditionally regarded public administration as gender neutral and had not paid close attention to the gender outcomes of policies or programmes. At the beginning, a number of departments, particularly the economic departments, believed that because their programmes were addressing the economy as a whole, their impact on men and women would be the same. For example, in 1985 the Department of Industry, Technology and Commerce claimed that because its programmes were intended to enhance Australia's economic perform-ance they "*therefore* equally impact on women and men" (emphasis added). The Department added that its programmes were "not aimed specifically at improving the status of women nor at maintaining or increasing the number of women employed" (OSW, 1985: 200).

Many public servants had never stopped to think that, because of the different roles performed by women and men in the economy and in the family, and the relationship between women's paid and unpaid work, the impact of public policy on them would be different. Because of the high degree of sex-segmentation of the Australian labour market, policies that benefited male employment might do nothing to help women. In fact, up until the 1980s job creation and labour market training programmes rarely benefited women, although female unemployment rates were consistently higher than those for men. Because women performed unpaid roles as primary carers of young, old or disabled family members, they tended to have different work histories from men, to spend more time at home and to be more vulnerable to poverty. The economic contribution of women's unpaid work is now sometimes recorded in satellite national accounts based on time-use surveys (Australian Bureau of Statistics (ABS), 1994), but too often its public policy consequences have been ignored.

The great virtue of the women's budget process was that departments could not escape for long with unsubstantiated claims that their policies and programmes were gender neutral. With the support of the Secretaries' Taskforce, the OSW insisted that supposed neutrality be demonstrated through disaggregated analysis of the effects of policies. This brought home to politicians and bureaucrats that few, if any, programmes and services were in reality gender neutral.

The pilot women's budget in 1984 generally focused on gender-specific services for groups such as war widows, or on the proportion of female clients of any given programme. The Social Security contribution was exceptional in its analysis of why, for example, the Commonwealth Rehabilitation Service had failed to make itself sufficiently accessible to women in the past. This had happened because they did not view unpaid household work as employment for which rehabilitation was appropriate.

47

As all agencies became accountable for the gender equity of outcomes, more attention was given to reasons for the differential impact of mainstream policies on women. This was important because specific programmes aimed at improving the economic and social status of women in the community constituted only a very small fraction of the overall effect, both positive and negative, of budgetary decisions on women. An analysis of the 1986–87 South Australian women's budget showed that direct allocations to improve the status of women and girls amounted, on average, to only 0.75 per cent of the budget of the 26 participating agencies.

Breaking Down the Economy by Gender

At the Federal level, as at the State level, it was the economic departments which mounted most resistance to the gender analysis of budgetary allocations. Gender analysis had made fewer inroads into economics than into any other of the social sciences. The struggle with the economic departments was part of the broader struggle to extend the areas where gender analysis was regarded as legitimate.

The Treasury contributions to the women's budget provided a useful index of gradual inroads made by the demand for disaggregated analysis. In 1985 the Treasury claimed that, because its programmes were aimed at the management of the macro-economy, "their impact on any particular group cannot be readily assessed" (OSW, 1985: 295). This was a bold claim, given the disproportionate dependence of women on public expenditure for employment, services and income support. There have been consistent findings that policies of reducing public expenditure as a proportion of gross domestic product (GDP) have specific impacts on women because of this relationship with the public sector. The repeated claim by the Treasury in women's budget statements that it was unable to measure the relative burdens and benefits of macroeconomic decisions on the basis of gender became the object of scathing criticism by economists outside government (for example, Outhwaite et al, 1986: 20).

The 1985 Treasury contribution also lacked analysis of the differential impact of the taxation system on men and women, apart from the observation that the dependent spouse rebate "tends to be granted chiefly in respect of women". At a meeting of women's desk officers in early 1986 the Treasury representative stated that, because his department provided economic advice rather than administering policies or programmes, it was, by definition, gender-neutral. He gave as an example the "gender-neutrality of the dependent spouse rebate which is available to women and men". An OSW representative pointed out that, while this rebate was theoretically available to both women and men, it was not neutral in its impact as it operated as a workforce disincentive to women. The rebate was paid to any man whose wife was engaged full-time in household work on his behalf, regardless of whether or not there were dependent children.

By the time of the 1986 women's budget, the Treasury was able to state that 97 per cent of claims for the dependent spouse rebate were made by men. However, there was still no discussion of its controversial nature as a form of family unit taxation and as a disincentive for women's workforce participation. Moreover, the Treasury contribution passed up the opportunity to stress that, apart from this rebate, the Australian taxation system was largely based on the individual as unit of account. This had been the case since the 19ᵗʰ century, when the colonies first introduced their income taxes. It distinguished Australia from many other countries where the use of family unit taxation provided disincentives to women's workforce participation. The disincentives come from taxing the second earner at the higher marginal rate and depriving them of their own tax-free threshold which recognises the costs of going to work. A taxation system that encourages economic dependency on the part of women is likely to exacerbate the feminisation of poverty.

Increased sensitivity to issues of gender equity – or retreat in the face of a determined women's desk officer – was seen in the Treasury's contribution to the 1987 document. At last there was recognition of a point made for ten years in submissions on taxation from women's organisations: "The Dependent Spouse Rebate is of greater value than the Sole Parent Rebate even though it can be argued that the sole parent who works is liable for child-care costs and does not receive the benefit of domestic duties provided by a dependent spouse". The dependent spouse rebate was finally removed from the taxation system as a result of a 1993 Federal election commitment and was paid out as a cash benefit to primary carers. A new prime minister elected in 1996 had, however, a long-term commitment to family unit taxation. He increased the tax threshold of taxpayers who had a partner full-time in the home and later provided a tax rebate for mothers who stayed at home full-time after childbirth.

The Department of Industry, Technology and Commerce was one

economic department that became persuaded of the disproportionate impact on women of macroeconomic reform. Considerably less had been spent by government on industry adjustment for the feminised textiles, clothing and footwear industries than for the male-dominated motor vehicle industry. While women, many of whom were migrants, accounted for 65 per cent of clothing workers, men accounted for over 80 per cent of employees in the motor vehicle industry (OSW, 1986: 178–82). A special retraining allowance was announced in 1987 for married women clothing workers who would otherwise have been ineligible on the grounds of their spouse's income.

Mandarin or Missionary Approach?

Anne Summers has described the Australian women's budget as "an example *par excellence* of the mandarin approach to women's policy" (Summers, 1986: 66). In other words, it was a bureaucratic rather than a community-based strategy. Nonetheless the women's budget was made widely available to women's organisations in 1985 and 1986. Defective women's budget reports were singled out in the assessment of ministers presented by a senator at the 1986 National Labour Women's Conference. Otherwise there was little media attention and the information the reports contained was not widely used by women's organisations or by academic experts. As noted, there was a shift in 1987 to a restricted print run of the full document. Apart from the forbidding size and turgidity of the full women's budget document, there were at least three reasons for its neglect by non-governmental organisations (NGOs).

The first reason was the lack of cross-portfolio analysis. In order for the women's budget process to succeed as an awareness-raising exercise, departments had to be given ownership of it. Individual portfolios have always prepared contributions to Australian women's budgets, although in accordance with centrally provided guidelines. This more or less excluded any real analysis of the cumulative impact of decisions across different portfolios. Australia has many community-based bodies which are publicly funded to perform representational and advocacy work on behalf of sections of the community that are poorly represented through parliaments, such as women. These bodies have often been more effective in identifying cross-portfolio impacts on their constituencies. The Women's Electoral Lobby, the Australian Council of Social Service or the National Council of Single Mothers and their Children have often been quick to pin-point the cumulative impact of cost-cutting exercises and the interaction of social security and taxation provisions in creating poverty traps.

A second reason for neglect was the women's budget's weakness in recording new budget decisions impacting on women. In recent years many decisions on the revenue side of the budget have been made by the Expenditure Review Committee of Cabinet only at the very last minute, after some testing of their political sensitivity through selective leaks. Because of this, and because of the intense time pressures of the whole budget process, women's desk officers often found out about decisions too late to include them. This pattern was also a reflection of the continuing tendency to allocate the women's budget responsibility at an insufficiently senior level. This contributed to the weakness of women's budgets in providing analysis of decisions made on the revenue side, as contrasted with the expenditure side of the budget.

Examples of 1986 budget decisions made too late to appear in the women's budget include wage discounting disproportionately impacting on low wage women; increased indirect tax on household items; a 25 per cent cut to the Human Rights Commission; and the loss of the Special Broadcasting Service. The last decision particularly affected migrant women at home and was eventually overturned after a successful campaign. Other 1986 decisions that got into the women's budget, but too late for gender analysis, included an up-front administration fee for tertiary students, which particularly affected married women without an independent income; a number of cuts to social security, exacerbating poverty traps for sole parents; and a major cut to the Community Employment Program, in which women had been over 50 per cent of participants.

A third reason for neglect of the women's budget documents by NGOs might be the cognitive dissonance created by the inclusion from 1986 of an introductory section justifying the government's economic strategy for dealing with the current account 'crisis'. Many disagreed with the assumptions that public investment 'crowded out' private investment or that the best way to solve overseas debt was to reduce domestic consumption, a strategy that meant less disposable income for those most in need, particularly those with children.

Nonetheless, the women's budget process did generate some internal pressure. One example is a statement in the 1986 Foreign Affairs contribution under the heading '1986/87 Expenditure Reductions':

> Significant reductions in the level of overseas development assistance are likely to have a disproportionately adverse impact on women's participation in development activities, if only because such cuts have an especially strong influence on new Initiatives and other discretionary areas of the aid budget (OSW, 1986: 136).

This cautious language was sufficient to alert the wise. Women benefited disproportionately more from the more discretionary areas of the aid budget, such as contributions to multilateral agencies, than from the bilateral agreements with regional governments. The cuts removed completely Australia's contribution to the UN Development Fund for Women (UNIFEM) and reduced the contribution to the UN Fund for Population Activities (UNFPA) by 78 per cent. With the help of the Status of Women Committee of the Parliamentary Labour Party and the National Women's Consultative Council, femocrats were able to make such a fuss about women having to bear the brunt of the cuts that funding was largely restored in the next budget.

Despite the careful official language required by a document cleared through departmental heads and ministers, and despite the failure at the Federal level to institutionalise reporting of performance against objectives, there survived the occasional comment revealing a mismatch between government policies and status of women objectives. In the 1986 women's budget the Health contribution noted that, while there was a general increase in breastfeeding, more needed to be done among Aboriginal women, recent migrants and poorer women:

> Social programmes to protect breast-feeding, for example, paid maternity leave for all workers and work-place childcare have not yet been fully addressed (OSW, 1986: 147).

In the Employment and Industrial Relations contribution we find the following:

> Women, who predominate in low-paid occupations and areas with lower levels of industrial activity, have benefited from wage indexation which has increased wages approximately every six months in line with changes in the inflation rate. The wage indexation guidelines have, however, contributed to maintaining existing wage relativities (OSW, 1986: 107).

For the women's budget process to become truly effective in reorienting government policy, it needs to be widely used as a yardstick of government performance, not only by those within government with responsibility for, or commitment to, equity issues, but also by community organisations, academics and the media. So far, this has not happened in Australia to any significant extent. In part this may be because of the dual functions performed by women's budget documents and the consequent effects on credibility. The Federal government document became increasingly less critical and more an exercise in departmental self-justification. The longer version never achieved an accessible style and the shorter version also failed to catch people's attention. One alternative is for gender budgets to be prepared independently of government, as has been the case in South Africa and the United Kingdom. However, this has the disadvantage of lack of access to confidential budget information. It also cannot perform the coordination and gender-awareness training functions for public servants of the model internal to government.

Following the Federal Lead

One advantage of federal systems is the scope they provide for policy experimentation and subsequent policy borrowings by other jurisdictions. The regular but informal meetings of Federal and State women's advisers were ideal forums for sharing policy experience and for policy transfer of successful experiments. All the States and Territories followed the Federal government in preparing women's budgets in varied forms. In historical order they were: Western Australia (1985), South Australia (1985), Victoria (1986), Australian Capital Territory (1989), New South Wales (1990), Queensland (1991), Tasmania (1991) and Northern Territory (1993). As noted, discussions of the women's budget idea originally took place at Federal/State women's adviser meetings. The South Australian adviser articulated most clearly that the function of the women's budget process was:

> ... to obtain information about what is being done for women, to raise the profile of women's programmes in bids for funding, but also to build into each Department a clear awareness that everything they do, every dollar they spend, has an impact on women – and that impact is often very different for women than for men (Treloar, 1987: 11).

These words were still being quoted in the Victorian women's budget in 1992. Both South Australia and Victoria developed comprehensive women's budget processes of similar scope to those at Federal government level and the discussion below focuses on these. Australia's other States and Territories developed their own women's budget processes. However, as the Director of Women Tasmania lamented, agency understanding of the crucial difference between gender neutrality and gender blindness often remained low (Buza, 1999).

The States' approach differed from that of the Federal government in that they tended to include data on public sector equal employment opportunity programmes. At the Federal level OSW wanted to dispel confusion between the external equity function – assessing the impact of government activity on women – and the internal equity function of equal employment opportunity. OSW guidelines therefore prevented departments including material about the latter, though they often tried to do so.

South Australia

Initiated in 1985, the South Australian women's budget had the most intellectual clarity, for which economist Rhonda Sharp was largely responsible. Analysis of expenditure was set out under the separate headings of 'Specifically Targeted Allocations to Women and Girls' and 'General Allocations – Impact of Key Activities on Women and Girls'. The document always began with an outline of the parameters of women's disadvantage. For example, in 1988 it stated that relevant factors in South Australia included the following:

◆ Over 100,000 women in the labour force have dependent children for whom they are the primary caregiver.

◆ Almost 90% of single parent families with dependent children are headed by women and 30% of single parent families live in poverty.

◆ Some 96% of families living below the poverty line are headed by women.

◆ Women comprise 77% of social security beneficiaries; twice as many women as men are solely dependent on the old age pension for income.

◆ Women comprise over 60% of the aged population 65 years and over and a greater proportion of those 75 years and over. Aged women are particularly vulnerable to poverty.

◆ Women comprise approximately 40% of the workforce. The

participation rate of women has increased by over 2% in the last year, with the greatest growth in part-time employment – more than 80% of part-time and casual workers are women. While part-time work suits women with family responsibilities, it is characterised by lower wages, less secure working conditions and limited promotional opportunities.

◆ The majority of women are employed in a narrow range of industries and occupations, with over 60% working in lower paid clerical, sales and service areas. Most professional workers in the 'caring' occupations such as nursing and children's services are women. Women's earnings averaged 66% of male weekly total earnings, a welcome but marginal improvement from 65% in 1987.

◆ Women constitute over 70% of the estimated 'hidden unemployed', i.e. those that are not included in the Australian Bureau of Statistics (ABS) definition of unemployed, such as discouraged job seekers. The estimated number of women who are hidden unemployed is 39,800 or 7.1% of all women aged over 15 years. Unemployment is highest among young women in the 15–19 age group (adapted from Government of South Australia, 1988: 4–5).

These introductions are a useful reminder of the rationale for disaggregated analysis. They also provide the background information as to why apparently neutral policies are likely to have a disparate impact. A good example is policies related to public transport, an area of government activity specific to State governments. Women are more dependent on public transport than are men, constituting in South Australia about 62 per cent of all passengers and 66 per cent of passengers in off-peak travel time. "Because women's work patterns and domestic responsibilities tend to be different to men's, their public transport needs are different – women go to different places at different times of the day" (Government of South Australia, 1990: 3). Access to transport is one of the major concerns for women working full-time in the home. Disaggregated analysis is extremely important in ensuring that moves to increase cost efficiency in public transport do not decrease women's access to it. This could happen through concentration on peak hour services on major commuter routes and a decrease in less profitable local services.

The South Australian women's budgets emphasised the international context. This ranged from the State's endorsement of International Labour Organisation (ILO) Convention 156 on Workers with Family

Responsibilities long before it was ratified by the Federal government to support for the UN International Year of Indigenous People through a special focus on Aboriginal women. The section on Aboriginal Women in the 1988 document again began by setting out very specifically the parameters of disadvantage:

> Aboriginal women… have a life expectancy approximately 20 years less than that of non-Aboriginal women, are three times more likely to die in childbirth and their children are 3–4 times more likely to die before their first birthday than non-Aboriginal children (Government of South Australia, 1988: 7).

The international context was also invoked in the discussion of women's unpaid work and its contribution to the economy. South Australia's 'public' economy is supported by work done largely by women in the domestic sphere, in rearing and caring for families and relatives, on farms, in local communities and in a wide range of voluntary activities. The 1985 UN Nairobi Forward Looking Strategies for the Advancement of Women, endorsed by Australia, urged that all countries begin to acknowledge women's contribution by assessing the value of household work in their national accounts. In comparable economies unpaid work has been estimated at between one-third and one-half of gross national product (GNP) (Government of South Australia, 1988: 2).

Despite the analytic edge of the South Australian exercise, it achieved a high degree of acceptance while backed by a Premier who also held the Treasury portfolio. A substantial section of the Treasury Circular concerning the preparation of the 1988–89 budget was devoted to it and to the need for agencies to evaluate activities in terms of outcomes for women. From 1989 agencies were expected to set longitudinal performance indicators for both their general and targeted programmes. These would measure, for example, the effectiveness of programmes in improving women's employment status. As elsewhere, however, the economic departments provided most resistance and there was at first little real gender analysis of industry assistance or investment attraction programmes.

One feature of the South Australian women's budget which was later copied in other States was the tracking of implementation of government policy on the appointment of women to government boards and committees across the different portfolios. This was not done at the Federal government level. However, the 1988 women's budget revealed that 84 per cent of those serving on government-appointed bodies in Foreign Affairs and Trade were men (OSW, 1988: 178).

The South Australian women's budget exercise fell victim to a change of government in 1993. The new conservative government maintained an emphasis on "recognising women as a discrete group of customers". However, it did not wish to maintain the previous accountability for expenditure. The idea of evaluating government responsiveness to women in terms of customer service was in itself an interesting indicator of the increased influence of private sector models. The incoming government argued that, while the women's budget had been an important initiative, its focus on financial allocations did not provide an adequate mechanism for monitoring achievements because these might only involve minimal cost. (Laidlaw, 1996: 1–2). The argument that real achievements for women might be so cheap as not to be worth accounting for in budgets may have been convenient for a government making drastic cuts in public expenditure. Reporting on specific initiatives for women, or so-called 'best practice' examples, was substituted for scrutiny of budget impact.

Victoria

The Victorian women's budget was initiated in 1986 and was largely modelled on the South Australian version. One major departure from both the Federal government and South Australian prototypes was the decision not to make it a formal budget document tabled on budget night. The argument was that it would attract more attention if launched separately from the budget. This would also enable control to be retained by the Women's Policy Coordination Unit. At the Federal government level there were continuing discussions with women's desk officers over this point. The conclusion there was that the exercise needed to remain integrated with the formal budget process, despite the drawbacks, in order to avoid marginalisation.

By 1988 the Victorian Women's Policy Coordination Unit had achieved clear endorsement from the Premier of their right to exercise editorial control so that the document would be clearly targeted to women in the community and to ministers. The resultant clear and consistent format enabled ready comparisons of performance across portfolios. The Victorians were also able to use a much more colourful and inviting format than the Federal government or South Australia, and their report was more often used than the others by politicians and trade union officials.

In the first year most of the work of preparing agency contributions was done by equal employment opportunity (EEO) officers. Subsequently chief executives of agencies were asked to select a women's budget programme liaison officer. It was made clear that EEO officers, who were part of the human resource management function rather than the policy side, were inappropriate. By 1988 an increased number of agencies had also appointed women's policy advisers and women's policy expertise was increasing. There were, however, the customary initial problems that departments did not have gender-specific data and needed help to get their data into reasonable shape.

The quality of the Victorian document improved each year. When launching the 1987 women's budget, the Premier held up to ridicule the quality of some agency contributions. The Department of Agriculture and Rural Affairs was mortified by the Premier's reference to its entry on the proportion of women in discussion groups on goat breeding in a country town. It had only been able to identify AUS$100 out of a AUS$50 million budget that directly benefited women. The department had targeted its activities to men, unaware that women were by and large the bookkeepers on farms or that a significant proportion of farm managers were women with children. The following year the department announced that a farming women's officer would be appointed to increase the participation of women in the department's programmes and ensure that the nature of women's role in agriculture was better understood within the department.

The Victorian women's budget, like its counterparts elsewhere apart from the Federal government, began by setting out the dimensions of female disadvantage, in a section entitled 'The Economic Status of Women in Victoria'. As in South Australia, each agency contribution was then clearly divided between 'specific allocations to benefit women' and 'general allocations and their impact on women'. Similarly also, the Victorian Women's Policy Coordination Unit assisted departments to develop performance indicators to measure the benefit of their activities for women. Both the South Australian and Victorian documents outstripped the Federal government prototype. The Victorian document was used by both backbenchers and ministers as a source of information, as well as by unions and community groups such as women's services. A readership survey in 1989 ensured continued attention to the accessibility of the document and avoidance of bureaucratic jargon.

Unlike in South Australia, the Victorian Women's Budget exercise survived the election of a conservative government in 1992. The presentation of the document continued to improve with, for example, graphically presented data on client profiles for each agency and on the representation of women on boards and committees and in the senior executive service. Client profile data in the 1993 document highlighted the fact that women were the major users of government-provided and government-subsidised cultural facilities, including the National Gallery of Victoria, State museums, public libraries, and music, dance and theatre (Office of Women's Affairs, 1993: 89).

However, by 1995 the client profiles provided for each agency had turned, as in South Australia, into 'customer profiles'. This was true even for agencies such as prisons or for groups such as victims of crime. The fact that women are only five per cent of 'customers' of the prison service has sometimes meant their needs are overlooked. Also, after the change of government the distinction between specific programmes for women and the impact of general programmes on women was no longer maintained. The focus shifted, apart from the customer and EEO data, to policies and initiatives of 'particular importance to women'. The 1996 guidelines for departments did, however, continue to emphasise the central purpose of the exercise as "a mechanism for government to report and be accountable to the community on outcomes for women" (Office of Women's Affairs, 1996: 1). And the outcomes selected had never been more clearly presented in pie charts and other graphics.

The Fate of Women's Budgeting

In general, the women's budget process would have been enhanced if community groups had been able to use the resulting documents as a lever when lobbying governments. The format of the Federal government version in particular, as a difficult-to-read budget document, militated against its use by NGOs. While it was shaped more as an internal accountability document, there was insufficient parliamentary oversight to prevent it becoming a public relations exercise rather than a useful analysis of the implications of budgetary allocations for women. It was also insufficiently linked into discourse about 'transparency in government', unlike the Victorian version which survived the election of a conservative and private sector-oriented government, although not indefinitely.

While policy learning between different levels of government had taken place at an early stage, the Federal government did not subsequently learn from the more successful State versions of women's budgeting. Nor was external advice sought from, for example, the Auditor General or a parliamentary committee, on how to develop the methodology for more effective gender reporting.

The Australian women's budget programme was a 'world first' in terms of asking bureaucrats to disaggregate the impact of their mainstream programmes rather than simply highlighting programmes for women. It had considerable influence at the international level. The first women's budget was tabled to great acclaim at a meeting of the Organisation for Economic Cooperation and Development (OECD) Working Party on Women and the Economy in February 1985. In 1987, the OSW gave presentations on it to a UN seminar on national machineries in Vienna and to the Harare meeting of Commonwealth Ministers Responsible for Women's Affairs. In 1998 it was selected as an example of best practice by a UN expert group meeting on national machineries for gender equality. (United Nations Division for the Advancement of Women, 1998). By 2001, gender budgeting initiatives of one sort or another had been attempted in more than 40 countries (Sharp and Broomhill, 2002).

Even as the women's budget idea was being taken up overseas, time was running out for the Australian prototype. Changes to the format of budgetary reporting sometimes made it difficult to pinpoint allocations and their impact. The cumulative effect of changes in budget methodology, changes in government and decreased resources due to cuts in the public sector brought about the gradual phasing out of women's budget processes. In 1993 a review recommended that it be replaced by two other accountability mechanisms. First, OSW was to share the cost of a five-person women's statistic unit in the Australian Bureau of Statistics that would publish benchmark data in an annual women's statistical yearbook. This would take the place of the gender equality indicators published in the women's budget statement since 1990 to measure outcomes of the government's efforts to improve the status of women. The second replacement mechanism was the inclusion of gender reporting in the programme statements provided annually by departments for scrutiny by parliamentary estimates committees and integration of gender equity criteria into programme targets.

The proposal that the women's budget statement disappear completely was temporarily thwarted by the intervention of the Status of Women Committee of the Parliamentary Labour Party. A very slim version of the statement appeared in 1994 and 1995. However, the formal requirement for gender reporting in programme performance statements provided to parliament has never occurred. Instead the format of budgetary reporting became more difficult to analyse in terms of gender impact. In 2000 a decision was taken which was of great consequence to women, namely reduction in entitlement to child support where a child was with a non-custodial parent for as little as one day a week. As was finally revealed in Senate Estimates, the decision had been taken without any research into its potential impact on sole parent poverty. No modelling had been done in the portfolio where the decision was taken and no analysis of this issue had been provided by OSW.

A 40 per cent cut to OSW in 1996 also swept away the women's statistics unit in the Australian Bureau of Statistics. Paradoxically, this cut could not be seen in the budget, although it was disproportionate to the cut in the rest of the portfolio. Other subsequent statistical losses included the downgrading of the national time-use survey from its status as a five-yearly social survey.

Under the new Federal government OSW was compelled to announce that:

> …while the innovative women's budget statement has been a valuable formal reporting mechanism, its purpose has been principally one of communication, with little impact on policy formulation. The strategic policy development and advising role, though a less public function of OSW, is a far more effective channel for the integration of gender issues into specific policies (OSW, 1996: 1).

Of course, the women's budget process had never been an *alternative* to policy advice and monitoring of Cabinet submissions. Further, as seen in relation to the child support changes, OSW was no longer able to moderate decisions detrimental to women.

Following the Federal lead again, other jurisdictions ceased preparing women's budgets. In New South Wales it was argued that the trend towards budgetary allocations being at a very high level of generality and aggregation meant extracting the relevant information was more difficult. Some femocrats believed it was no longer a cost-effective means of going about gender accountability. They felt that while the women's budget process initially provided important insights, these insights were not proportionately extended by the annual repeat of such a resource-intensive exercise.

Some thought the yardstick of budgetary allocations did not put sufficient emphasis on outputs or outcomes as contrasted with inputs. Others pointed to the competing objectives that the women's budgets tried to serve and decided that these might be reached more effectively in other ways. For example, focus groups in Queensland suggested that the community information function might better be met by targeted leaflets on specific policy areas and through an annual economic and social profile providing longitudinal data. Similarly, the accountability function might be achieved by including data on women as clients in budgetary documents, strategic plans and annual reports (*Women's Word: Journal of the Women's Policy Unit, Office of the Cabinet* March 1995: 14). Some jurisdictions such as New South Wales introduced, as a replacement for the women's budget, annual audits of government programmes assessing performance against election commitments to women on the one hand, and the Convention on the Elimination of All Forms of Discrimination against Women (CEDAW) and the Beijing Platform for Action on the other.

Such initiatives have not filled the accountability gap left by the demise of the women's budget process. For example, at the Federal government level the OSW has lost the coordinating role the gender budget gave it. It has also lost the mandate to advise all departments on the kind of data needed for gender accountability. And it has lost the working relationship with the economic departments that women's budgeting requires – although, as we have seen, without strong political will the economic departments tend to resist the methodology of gender budgeting. Less gender-disaggregated data is being maintained by departments and it is often only produced as a result of questions at Senate Estimates hearings. There has also been a loss of expertise within departments concerning what is potentially a gender issue. Overall the information about the implications for women of budgetary allocations is much more fragmented. Stronger parliamentary oversight, particularly where parliamentary committees are relatively independent of government control, is necessary to ensure continuing effectiveness of internal accountability mechanisms. Bodies reporting to parliament, such as Auditors General, might also play a role in ensuring that government agencies are producing clear information on budgetary allocations and who benefits from them.

In 2001 the Australian Labor Party committed itself to the reintroduction of gender budgeting at the Federal level but failed to win the elections. In the meantime community-based gender audits have achieved some successes in Victoria. Today gender auditing in government remains an important tool of gender mainstreaming in Australia at the State and Territory level, although without the formal ties to the budget or emphasis on the impact of across-the-board budget allocations.

References

Australian Bureau of Statistics (ABS) (1994). "Unpaid Work and the Australian Economy 1992." ABS, Canberra

Buza W. (1999). "Women Tasmania Discussion Paper on Options to Replace the Women's Budget Statement."

Government of South Australia (1985–93). *The Budget and its Impact on Women.* Government Printer, Adelaide.

Laidlaw D. (1996). Ministerial Statement, 27 November.

Office of the Status of Women (OSW) (1984–85). *Women's Budget Program 1984–85; 1985–86.* Australian Government Publishing Service (AGPS), Canberra.

_____ (1986–95). *Women's Budget Statement 1986–87, 1987–88 etc.* Australian Government Publishing Service (AGPS), Canberra.

_____ (1996). "Gender Integration into Macro-Economic Policies and the Federal Budget Process in Australia." Paper prepared for the Fifth Meeting of Commonwealth Ministers Responsible for Women's Affairs, Trinidad & Tobago, 25–28 November.

Office of Women's Affairs (1993–1996). *Victoria Women's Budget 1993–94 etc* Melbourne: Office of Women's Affairs, Dept of Justice, Victoria.

_____ (1996). "Guidelines for Development of 1996–97 Women's Budget Entries," Office of Women's Affairs, Dept of Justice, Victoria.

Outhwaite S., M. Power & S. Rosewarne (1986). "Writing Women out of the Economy." Paper presented for the Australia and New Zealand Association for the Advancement of Science Centenary Conference, Sydney, 17 May.

Sawer M. (1990). *Sisters in Suits: Women and Public Policy in Australia.* Sydney, Allen & Unwin.

Sharp, R. and R. Broomhill (2002). 'Budgeting for Equality: The Australian Experience' in *Feminist Economics* 8 (1).

Summers A. (1986). "Mandarins or Missionaries: Women in the Federal Bureaucracy" in N. Grieve and A. Burns (eds). *Australian Women: New Feminist Perspectives*. Melbourne, Oxford University Press.

Treloar C. (1987). Speech to Women's Information Services National Conference, Alice Springs, 5–7 May.

United Nations Division for the Advancement of Women (1998). Report: National Machineries for Gender Equality: Expert Group Meeting, Santiago, Chile. UNDAW, New York.

Women's Word: Journal of the Women's Policy Unit, Office of the Cabinet, Queensland, March 1995.

Korea: Raising questions about women-related policies

Yoon Jung Sook

Table 4: Selected Indicators for Korea

Indicator	*Year*	*Number*
Population	2000	45,985,000
% of population which is female	2000	49.8%
% of population which is urban	1999	9.0%
Gross domestic production (GDP) per capita(US$)	1999	15,712
Human development index (HDI)	1999	0.875
Gender development index (GDI)	1999	0.868
% of total budget funded by donors	2002	0
% of national parliamentarians who are women	2000	5.9%

Introduction

Korea's first gender budget project

During 2001, the Korean non-governmental organisation (NGO) WomenLink carried out a gender budget analysis of seven local governments. WomenLink had been established in 1987 to promote grassroots women's participation in eleven regions of the country. Today it is one of the largest and most active Korean women's NGOs and works in the areas of family and sexuality, labour rights, media action, environment and political empowerment. The gender budget work is part of its political empowerment focus. The analysis was undertaken over nine months, from April until December, and was the first time that women's policies were analysed from this perspective in Korea.

The concept of gender budgeting is not yet well known in Korea beyond a few researchers. This has resulted in insufficient specialists in this area, a lack of development of methods and a shortage of instruments. Given these conditions, WomenLink began the analysis of budgets by studying the gender impact of women-related policies.

The project was named "Establishing a new paradigm for local governments' women policies and budget analysis" and was implemented in local governments where WomenLink's head office and branch offices are located. These included two large-unit local governments in Seoul City and Kangwon province, and five basic-unit local governments in Wonju City, Goyang City, Jinju City, Dobong Gu and Yangchon Gu in Seoul. The project drew a lot of attention and interest from women's groups, civil society organisations, local governments, local assemblies and the Ministry of Gender Equality.

The project was implemented by activists and members of WomenLink together with researchers, and was supported by funds from the Ministry of Government and Home Affairs. Under the 1999 Civil Society Organisation Support Act, this Ministry is responsible for allocating funds to NGOs for specific thematic projects. All the participants worked as volunteers with no compensation.

The First Basic Plan on Women's Development

The adoption of gender mainstreaming as one of the nation's policies in 1995 had a significant influence on the systematisation of Korea's women-related policies. In 1995 the government passed the Framework Act on Women's Development. This law states that the aims of women's policies are to (a) promote equality between men and women; (b) expand women's social participation; and (c) increase women's welfare. It was under this law that the first Basic Plan of Women Policies (1998–2002) was established. The plan consisted of six key strategies, 20 policy goals and 144 specific goals. The key strategies and policy goals are shown in Table 5. The law requires that the national and local governments take appropriate measures to implement the First Basic Plan.

Table 5: First Basic Plan of Women Policies

Key Strategy	*20 Policy goals*
Reform laws, systems and customs and women's representation	1. Change gender discriminatory laws and preconceptions 2. Expand women's participation in the policy decision-making process
Support and stabilise women's employment	3. Build a foundation for gender equal chances in employment

	4. Support women's employment
	5. Establish a system to support work and household management
	6. Improve working conditions for women
Establish an educational system that facilitates women's competitive advantage	7. Create conditions for gender equal education
	8. Educate women professional human resources
	9. Support lifetime education for women
Develop welfare services for women and families	10. Improve women's health and balance the gender ratio
	11. Expand and improve the child-care system
	12. Support the interests of women agricultural workers
	13. Enhance the degree of welfare for women needing care
	14. Increase welfare for elderly women
	15. Eradicate violence against women
Build a foundation for women's cultural and social activities	16. Expand women's cultural activities
	17. Support volunteer and civil movements
	18. Support the activities of women's organisations
Expand women's participation in international cooperation and the unification of Korea	19. Strengthen international cooperation among women
	20. Contribute to the unification of Korea

Establishment of women's focal points and a gender ministry

The Kim Dae-jung administration took office in February 1998 and established the Presidential Commission for Women's Affairs under the direct authority of the President. The Government also set up so-called Women's Focal Points in six ministries, namely the Ministries of Justice, Labour, Health and Welfare, Agriculture and Forestry, Education and Human Resources, and Government and Home Affairs. The mandate of these gender experts is to build a cooperative system with other departments in their respective ministries to deal with women-related policies.

In 2001, the government extended and reformed the Presidential

Commission for Women and established it as the Ministry of Gender Equality. The Government charged the new Ministry with developing an administrative system for mainstreaming women-related policies. The local provincial governments also established or reformed the departments of women-related policies. Under the Framework Act on Women's Development, the central and local governments are required to report annually on their plans for and implementation of women-related policies to the Ministry of Gender Equality.

As a result of this law, both the central and local governments increased their interest in policies concerning women and established (admittedly small) Women's Development Funds in order to support women-related projects in their region. There has thus been a positive change. However, there has been no evaluation of the implementation of women-related policies due to the absence of evaluation standards and the lack of an ability to evaluate.

Furthermore, officials' understanding of gender issues is weak. Despite the implementation of a gender sensitivity training programme, many officials in charge of women-related policies are not familiar with the concepts of gender main streaming and gender budgeting. Insufficient recognition on the part of officials and the absence of an evaluation system are affecting women-related policies as well as more general policy and budget decision-making processes both directly and indirectly.

An inadequate gender-specific budget

Gender mainstreaming was selected as a key strategy in the national policy and administrative system for women-related policies. However, the budget allocation provides evidence of several problems. In the case of the central government, the budget for the Ministry of Gender Equality for 2001 was only 0.003 per cent of the total general account. Further, the total budget allocated for the Ministry of Gender Equality, as well as women-targeted programmes in seven ministries and the Small and Medium Enterprises Department, was approximately 0.28 per cent of the national general account.

Several women's organisations pointed out that, because of the small budget, many projects could not achieve their targets. Women's organisations also criticised the insufficient budget and inefficient women-related policies as 'budget wasting' and demanded stronger authority for the Ministry of Gender Equality and women's bureaux in local governments as well as expanded budget and human resources. Moreover, they urged the government to consider establishing Women's Focal Points in all ministries.

WomenLink undertook the gender budget project as a first step in coming up with specific grounds for raising problems around the fairness and efficacy of women-related policies. The organisation also saw the project as providing the basis for counterproposals. This chapter looks at the process of this gender budget project and briefly examines the results of the analysis of women-related policies through a case study of one local government's gender-specific budget. Common results of the analysis of the budgets of other local governments are summarised later in the chapter as well as WomenLink's future plans.

Process: Training, Analysis and Feedback

Workshops and courses

Staff and members of WomenLink's head and branch offices analysed the budget and policies. In order to provide education to participants about the concept of gender mainstreaming, gender budgets and methods of analysis, several workshops were held. Women members of local assemblies and specialists participated in the workshops while staff and members of WomenLink played a central role. Advisory groups were set up, consisting of members of local assemblies, university professors, activists of civil budget inspection groups and lawyers.

Three workshops were held. The first workshop included a lecture and discussion about the basic tools of gender budget analysis. At the second workshop, participants presented their interim reports on the analysis of each local government's budget and policies. At the third workshop, participants presented the final results and drafted a written request to the government to introduce a gender perspective into their policy and budget-making processes.

Education courses of between four and eight sessions were also provided for local teams. Participants included staff and members of WomenLink who were to work on the analysis, activists from local women organisations and civil society groups. Subjects included the concept of gender mainstreaming, women-related policies and gender budgets, and the importance and method of budget analysis.

69

Assessing the health of current policies

All the members of WomenLink who participated in the analysis were organised under the name of 'Women's Group for Healthy Politics'. The group's name was abbreviated to 'Saengkang Women's Group'. The abbreviation 'Saengkang' has the same pronunciation as the Korean word for ginger, which is a common ingredient in Korean cooking and is supposed to eliminate bad smells, prevent colds, heal inflammations, facilitate blood circulation and relieve thirst. The name symbolises the function of the organisation.

The organisation, which had 40 members, undertook to engage in the following activities:

◆ analysing the local government's women-related policies and budget, and presenting a counterproposal every year,

◆ monitoring local assembly meetings, and

◆ meeting with heads and members of local self-governments to discuss gender budget demands.

Each branch of the Saengkang Women's Group invited local officials and members of the local assembly to a forum after they had done the analysis. Participants, who included members of women's organisations, civil society groups, the local assembly and other officials, had a lively discussion. They showed interest in the results, which were probably new for them. The national and local press reported on the forums.

Members of the Saengkang Women's Group of each branch office attended the assembly accounts and budget deliberation process for 2002. They handed over a short message with suggestions about women-related policies and budget planning as well as a flower symbolising encouragement. Reactions to the visit and the message were different in each area. In one local assembly, councillors accepted the results of the data analysis as requested and subsequently incorporated the suggestions in the budget for women-related policies of 2002. However, there were other local officials who did not accept the results and failed to take further action.

Disseminating the findings

The results of the analysis were published and distributed to women's organisations, civic groups, the Ministry of Gender Equality, heads of local governments, members of local assemblies, female members of the National Assembly and others. Each branch of WomenLink published a special paper, 'Local management by local citizens', which contained summarised results of the gender budget analysis of their local government's budget. The papers were distributed to local citizens, officials, members of the local assembly and the local press.

The results of the gender budget analysis of seven local governments together with common points were presented in a plenary session at a public forum, where a counterproposal was also suggested. Officials of central and local governments and specialists were invited as a panel and more than 100 people attended the discussion. Participants included members of women's organisations, civil society groups, officials of central and local governments, researchers and members of the press.

In order to further disseminate and share the results, WomenLink was involved in several meetings with civil groups and women's organisations. It also worked with the Budget Inspection Civil Group Network. Further, WomenLink presented a case study at several meetings including a local election candidate's workshop, where it discussed women-related local policies for the future. In addition, a discussion about the process of local government budget analysis was held with ten other local women's organisations.

WomenLink delivered the results of the analysis to the Government and presented them at a forum organised by the government's women's policy research institution, the KWDI. WomenLink also unofficially requested government bureaucrats to adopt the gender budget, develop methods of analysis, create educational programmes for activists from women's organisations and officials, and refer to the results of the analysis when establishing the Second Women's Development Plan (2003–2007). In the Ministry of Gender Equality's White Paper on Women-related Issues of 2002, the concept of gender budgeting was introduced for the first time and the budget amount for women-related policy was stated. The paper also stated that developing the budget from a gender-sensitive perspective would be necessary in the future.

Gender Budget and Policy Analysis

Methodology

WomenLink applied the following methods to evaluate the goals and contents of women-related policies using the gender budget concept.

◆ *Data about population and social conditions of local governments.* We collected basic data and statistics about population and women-related policies. These data provided a measure of women's demands and the range and number of beneficiaries.

◆ *Goals and focus of women-related policies.* We researched the goals and detailed programmes of women-related policies, what kind of projects are implemented and how they strive to pursue the goal in each local government.

◆ *Administrative system to enforce women-related policies.* We did research on the administrative system for women-related policies, its authority and the number of officials in charge to find out if the administrative system is suitable for implementing women-related policies efficiently. This aspect included the percentage of women officials and their distribution by rank, the percentage of women participating in each local government committee, and the regulations relating to women and the Women's Development Fund.

◆ *Analysis of budget and expenses.* We checked if the amount of the budget allocated for women-related policies was appropriate and if the budget was efficiently used. In particular, we looked at the proportion of the total budget allocated for women, then analysed items related to the goals of women-related policies and specific projects.

◆ *Funding and regulations.* We investigated whether regulations related to women existed and the amount of the Women's Development Fund.

◆ *Analysis of women-related policies and budget from a gender-sensitive perspective.* We researched the contents of women-related policies and the use of budgets for all women. In doing this, we found certain projects that violated the principle of gender equality.

Weaknesses and strengths

In our analysis we used data sources such as local government statements of accounts of tax revenue and expenditures, a white paper about women-related issues, documents about policy plans and the implementation of women-related policies by different departments, women-related statistics and detailed interviews of beneficiaries of the policies. Collecting the data was difficult because officials were reluctant to release this and were unresponsive to public requests for information. As a result, the information was collected through unofficial routes.

Our approach created complications with officials in some regions. When there were members of the local assembly or officials who understood the activities of the women's movement, the collection of information was easy. In some other cases, the data collection process took longer than the analysis. In the absence of gender-disaggregated data it was nearly impossible to carry out any substantial gender budget analyses.

We mainly analysed the parts of the budget classified as 'women policies' and then added other projects targeting or affecting women. As a result, the gender-specific aspects of the budget had priority in the analysis and other projects that were relevant to women-related policies were only selectively analysed. The analysis therefore does not give a full picture of the gender impact of the budget. An additional weakness was the lack of sophisticated methods of analysis.

The strength of the analysis was its ability to find out the gender impact of women-related policies and the implementation of women-targeted budgets. In addition, we learned about many aspects of the projects: whether they reinforced gender equality or solved the problems of gender-biased views and culture; whether the range of beneficiaries was appropriate; and whether the projects were effective in the long-term or should be revised.

The analysis also provides some pointers to whether the local governments' women policies and the budget were implemented properly and if budget planning was efficient. However, the project was limited to the analysis of budget and policies for women only, so that it provides insufficient analysis of the gender aspect of other budgets or policies.

Common Findings of the Analysis

◆ *Absolute shortage of budget.* In 2001, the budget for women-related policies of the seven local governments studied was very low, ranging between 0.1% and 2.3% of the general account. The allocations for the Women's Development Fund, which was provided for in the 1995 Basic Law of Women's Development, were also very small.

◆ *Lack of gender-dissagregated statistics.* Since there were almost no gender-disaggregated statistics, analysing the effect by gender was difficult and only a few programmes could be examined.

◆ *Insufficient gender perspective in budget and policies.* Usually the women-targeted budget was merely one component of broader social or family welfare programmes. Although the programme titles were similar to those of the central government and the Framework Plan on Women's Development, and exhibited a level of gender sensitivity, in reality many programmes did not really fulfil the purpose of gender equality promotion.

◆ *Weak administrative standardisation.* The authority, system, function and scale of the department in charge of women-related policies was different in each local government, as was the classification system of budget items. Although not problematic *per se*, these different administrative systems made the process of our analysis more difficult.

◆ *Planning based on the concept of 'marginalised women'.* The concept of 'marginalised women' is still officially used in Korean local governments. Since many women-related policies specifically target women who need protection, not all women are included in the policies.

◆ *Weak authority of women's policy departments.* The women-related policy implementing departments had small budgets and limited human resources and authority. However, we also learned that the relative influence of these women's policy bureaux depended partly on the political will of respective local government heads.

◆ *Low representation of women in the bureaucracy.* The percentage of women officials in local government is small and most remain in low ranks. Additionally, few women are members of local assemblies or advisory committees. This situation makes it difficult to establish a foundation for gender-sensitive women-related policies and budget planning.

Table 6 shows the percentage of women officials in each of the seven local governments studied. This is never higher than 30.3 per cent for women public officials of all ranks, 31.0 per cent for women members of ministerial advisory committees, and 5.3 per cent for women public officials in grades 5 and above, i.e. those in decision-making positions.

Table 6: Representation of women among public officials and appointed civilian members in local government bureau advisory committees (%)

Category	Seoul	Kangwon Province	Wonju City	Goyang City	Seoul Yangchon-Gu	Seoul Dobon-Gu	Jinju City
Bureaucrats	23.3	23.8	25.7	n/a	30.3	26.4	25.6
Grade 5 & higher	5.0	3.2	4.9	3.4	5.1	5.3	3.8
Members of advisory committees	31.0	19.9	30.3	17.8	21.7	11.0	8.6

As noted previously in the discussion of data collection, the officials in charge of women-related policies had a limited understanding and were often not willing to cooperate with civil society groups undertaking budget analysis. Some women-related policies demonstrated, or even strengthened, gender-biased views. The examples are:

◆ In Wonju City there was a special lecture at a 2001 Women's Fair entitled: 'A happy wife and a successful husband'. There was also a high school graduation preparatory training for girls involving make-up and skin care.

◆ In Jinju city the women's welfare budget funded a food bank project, a traditional food festival and women's education focusing on etiquette and family rituals.

◆ In Kangwon province there was a 'harmonious couple' award, the Shinsaim-dang award (see below) and an award for 'proud woman in Kangwon'.

◆ In Goyang City there was a 'Miss Flower' beauty contest

WomenLink in cooperation with two local NGOs is currently investigating budget wastage as well as discriminatory practices such as requesting beauty contest winners to serve as hostesses at meetings with important functionaries involved in the contests. According to our research there are approximately 100 such contests held nationally! We will hold a local hearing about these issues in July 2002.

Case Study of Kangwon Province

Background

Kangwon province is one of the 16 provincial and metropolitan city governments of Korea. The population is 1,556,979, of whom women represent just under 50 per cent. The percentage of women aged 65 years or older is 11.0 per cent, which is higher than the national average of 8.2 per cent (Department of Statistics, 2000).

Women's economic activity participation rate in Kangwon Province is 46.4 per cent, which is lower than the national average of 49.2 per cent, and considerably lower than men's: 70.9 per cent. However, the population of working elderly women is high, at 32 per cent of the total population of women engaged in economic activities. About three-quarters (73%) of women engaged in economic activities have only a primary or high school education. Approximately 16 per cent of the total female population is involved in agriculture.

The structures in charge of policies for women are the women-related policy office, which is directly responsible to the provincial governor, and the women's welfare section, which is part of the environment and welfare department. The women policy office is responsible for developing, managing and organising women-related policies. The women's welfare section operates women's welfare facilities, benefits for marginalised women such as prostituted, low-income or homeless women, and child-care support. This office and section use women's institutions as business centres. Some 48 officials, 24 men and 24 women, work for the department.

Women officials represent 21 per cent of all officials in the province. This is lower than the national average of 30 per cent, which is also the government's recommendation. The percentage of women officials who are at level 5 or higher is 3.1 per cent, which is much lower than the national average of 8.1 per cent.

The establishment of Regulations of a Special Committee for Women Policies in 1998 led to the formation of a Special Committee for

Women-related Policies which is an advisory structure for the provincial governor. There are also several regulations such as Regulations of Establishment and Operation of Funding for Women's Development (1997) and Shinsaim-dang Regulations (1987). The Regulations for Women's Development, which were based on the Basic Law of Women's Development are not active yet. The Women's Development Fund had accumulated 30 billion won by 2000. The Shinsaim-dang award is presented to a woman every year to pay tribute to Shinsaim-dang who is the symbolic figure of a sacrificing mother. The award emphasises the traditional female figure.

Goals and focus of women–related policies

The overall goals of Kangwon's women-related policies are to promote greater respect and opportunities for women, to improve the competitiveness of the women in Kangwon as important human resources and to create synergy between women and men in the 21st century.

More specifically, the goals are:

1. to promote policies to improve women's status and quality of life;
2. to reform gender discriminatory systems and customs;
3. to improve women's abilities and interests;
4. to encourage women's participation in society and social organisations;
5. to build a foundation for women's welfare;
6. to develop child-care services; and
7. to support the development of women agricultural workers and expand women's role.

We used these goals in analysing the budget, as shown below.

In evaluating the policies we found that:

◆ Programmes such as the protection of maternity, development of abilities and encouragement of social participation do not affect all women. Instead, they are focused on women and children who need protection. In addition, not all women are included as beneficiaries for capacity-building policies.

◆ Although a lower percentage of women than men are economically active, there are no policies to enhance women's employment. In addition, there are no specific goals in respect of the low employment of female college graduates. Practical policies for women agricultural workers are also lacking.

◆ Child-care plans are considered only for low-income families and children in need of protection. General measures for managing family and working conditions are insufficient.

Looking at the budget

The gender-specific budget includes allocations for women-related policies, women's welfare, children's welfare and the operation of women's institutions and training centres. The budget for women is part of the social welfare budget, which represented 6 per cent of the total budget for the year 2001. Within the social welfare budget, the budget for women-related policies was 0.1 per cent of the total, women's welfare was 0.1 per cent, child-care support 1.9 per cent, women's institutions 0.1 per cent and women's training centre management 0.0 per cent.

In terms of the first policy goal, enhancing women's social status and quality of life, five plans were proposed:

◆ To institute basic regulations to assure women's advancement,

◆ To increase women's participation in various committees,

◆ To increase the Women's Development Fund

◆ To review and evaluate women's policies and offer incentives

◆ To promote women' policy research and host discussion sessions.

The Women's Development Fund showed a slight increase from the year before. However, the outcomes of women's policy studies and conferences were not widely shared with Kangwon women's organisations or the female public at large. And it remains unclear how these research results are reflected in women's policies.

The introduction of a women's policy evaluation and an incentive system risks widening the gap between Kangwon and other local governments in terms of the implementation of women's policies. Another concern is that it could lead to an excessively competitive atmosphere in terms of handling projects. If the administration is to provide rewards to local governments which perform, the budget for that purpose should be allocated to programmes that have wider benefits for overall women's policies developed by all local or city governments.

In terms of policy goal 2, spreading equality by addressing gender-discriminatory institutions and practices, many projects did not have a budget. Where there were budgets, they were often too small, making the projects just 'feel-good' lip-service.

One of the programmes, Women's Sarangbang (guest room), is a venue to provide counselling to female public servants. Initially, the name was Equality Sarangbang. The new name obscures the purpose. The name change may have been brought about by a negative reaction to the term 'equality'.

In another programme, events organised during Women's Week have been only for small, government-friendly pockets of women's organisations. In the future, Women's Week should come up with activities to involve ordinary citizens regardless of their gender. Moreover, all the events need to be organised and led by women's organisations rather than by the government.

There were almost no projects in terms of policy goal 3, development of women's capabilities and empowerment. Further, the existing projects often had no budget. Women's continuing education projects were mostly designed for the leaders of women's organisations rather than for the general female public. Projects to 'uplift Kangwon women's spirit' were aimed at developing and disseminating an exemplary female role model, but the Shinsaim-dang Award may backfire by strengthening traditional stereotypes of women (see below).

There was not a single project in terms of the fourth policy goal, promotion of women's participation and revitalisation of organisations. The only item involved conversation sessions between women leaders, and education and events for volunteers. Projects such as the Millennium Renaissance Symbolism project, Winter Olympics and Kind, Orderly, Clean People Movement mainly concerned provincial government's activities. These activities are far removed from the policy goal of women's social participation.

Policy goal 5 involves women's welfare and sound child-rearing. Most of the interventions under this goal were for women in need of social protection. But the inclusion in 2001 of preventive programmes such as counselling courses and education programmes to prevent sexual assault are welcome.

A large proportion of the budget went into the construction of

women's centres. In Kangwon Province, 14 centres are in operation
with six more to be built so that all 18 cities and counties will have
one. However, given the trend of district or county administration
offices being transformed into 'local citizens' centres', it would be more
desirable to utilise existing facilities for welfare service purposes. This
will prevent squandering of financial resources.

When planning and implementing programmes for low-income single
parents or women in need of protection, policy makers should consider
the convenience of beneficiaries. With combined responsibilities of
job and child-rearing, they can not easily participate in long-term,
retreat job training courses. They need reimbursement for their
participation in job training as well as convenient conditions that
would enable them to go to the class. An increased budget is needed
to support after-class activities for low-income single parent families.
In addition, the sharp increase in single parent families points to the
need for programmes such as counselling services.

There are 561 child-care centres, which between them can
accommodate 23,257 children. This represents 55 per cent of a total of
42,398 children in need of child-care services. The number of
national, public or company facilities is only 57. Thus, on average,
each city or county has only three child-care centres provided by
public institutions.

Evaluating specific projects

Women's education: limited beneficiaries

Those who received training and education were mostly leaders or
members of women's organisations. Education programmes targeting
ordinary female employees were only held at the Kangwon Women's
Adult Education Centre. Since this was Korea's first video
conferencing system education programme, it attracted a lot of
attention. However, given the situation of ordinary women and their
daily lives, it is questionable whether a 12-week, lecture-oriented
video conferencing programme can ever be effective. Moreover, an
excessively large budget was allocated to the programme. It would be
far more cost effective and useful if women study-related lectures were
organised in each city or county, or if women's education programmes
were provided by local private women's organisations with government
support.

Awards that may strengthen stereotypical gender roles

The 'Harmonious Couple' award is given to a couple "who represent a model case in line with Kangwon peoples' moral standards and sentiment, and who have made a democratic and good family through mutual respect and cooperation". The title of the award was originally 'Equal Couple' but some people protested that the term 'equal' was not appropriate for husband and wife relations and so the name was changed. The first awardee was a couple from a traditional family. Although they were not a well-to-do family, the husband and wife supported their parents, brothers and sisters and raised four children successfully and happily. They have separate bank accounts and use honorific words to address each other. More weight, however, was placed on the woman's traditional virtues as daughter-in-law, wife and mother than on sharing household chores, equal decision making or sharing properties.

The Shinaim-dang award is named after a woman of that name who was from Kangwon Province and remains the symbol of 'Korean mothers with sublime wifely virtues'. Again, the woman is acclaimed for her virtues as mother and wife rather than as an individual with commendable virtues. This strengthens traditional gender stereotypes. Last year's awardee was a wife with seven sisters and brothers-in-law, who has served her mother and father-in-law well and raised her son to become a dean of a graduate school.

The 'Proud Kangwon Woman' award is for women who have 'made valuable contributions to women becoming part of the mainstream'. The 2001 award was given to a woman entrepreneur actively engaged in business activities, who had passed the bar exam with the highest scores.

Accomplishments and Limitations

WomenLink's analysis of seven local government budgets illustrates current problems in budget allocation as well as spending related to women-specific issues. It also shows the importance of gender-sensitive policy-making. Through the project, the need for gender-sensitive budget allocation and women's policy analysis was widely shared. The capacity to participate in women's policy making was also improved.

WomenLink members taking part in this analysis became more confident in their capacity to deal with regional women's policy-making processes. They formed women's groups under the name of 'Women's budget participation movement' or 'Local assembly monitoring movement' in their respective regions. Through case study presentations and discussion, the members shared information with other local citizens and women's organisations. Via these channels, regional branch offices of WomenLink began weaving a network, connecting civic and women's organisations for the analysis and monitoring of local government budgets.

WomenLink's activities captured the attention of the central government and local assembly members. Members demanded that the government and local assembly lawmakers take into consideration the results of their analysis in their policy-making, and drew attention to the importance of gender-sensitive budget and policy development. In 2002, the Ministry of Gender Equality announced that the development of tools to provide gender-sensitive budget analysis is an urgent need.

In addition, before the 2002 June local elections WomenLink and several civic groups distributed questionnaires about budget plans to Seoul City government candidates. WomenLink asked questions about their gender budget component. After analysing the responses to these questionnaires, they plan to pressure the successful candidates to keep to their pre-election promises.

One limitation, however, is that to date, the analysis has only covered gender-specific budgets and women's policy. It has stopped short of comprehensive gender-sensitive budget analysis. A lack of analytical tools and gender-dissagregated statistics did not permit a full analysis.

Future Plans

WomenLink sees pressure for gender budget analysis gaining nationwide momentum. Members will conduct analyses every year. In 2002, the plan is to expand their gender budget analysis to the central government level. In particular, the focus will be on the maternity-leave related budget of the Ministry of Labour.

In order to continually improve our analytical tools, WomenLink plans to form a network with experts and other women's groups. We will conduct training programmes for women activists on gender budget analysis, and pressure government agencies to provide sponsorship for these training sessions. We will carry out activities demanding gender budget measures by the central and local governments in cooperation with other women's groups and undertake lobbying activities to encourage the government to create a budget planning process that facilitates broader women's participation.

Mexico: Collaborating with a wide range of actors

Helena Hofbauer

Table 7: Selected Indicators for Mexico

Indicator	Year	Number
Population	2000	97,483,412
% of population which is female	2000	51%
% of population which is urban	1995	64%
Gross Domestic Project (GDP) per capita (US$)	1999	8297
Human development index (HDI)	1999	0.790
Gender development index (GDI)	1999	0.782
% of total budget funded by donors		n/a
% of national parliamentarians who are women	2002	16%

Introduction

This chapter describes the development of the Mexican gender budget initiative. The initiative started out as the effort of a nation-wide feminist network, integrated during its first years a research centre that specialised in budget analysis, and later on reached into governmental structures. Along the way, the initiative has incorporated experiences, efforts and the work of other networks and organisations, and inserted the topic of gender-sensitive budgets as an item in the political agenda. It has grown in strength due to its diversity, as well as by integrating two essential components in a primarily political endeavour. These elements are the active advocacy capacities of women's organisations and the solid technical skills of a policy research centre.

The first part of the chapter describes the way in which the initiative came together, in order to illustrate the strength of the groups behind it and the dynamic of the process. The second part focuses on the change in government and the way in which the reconfiguration of the political agenda was used to advance the initiative. The third part describes how collaboration with a selected sector, the Department of Health, has increased the scope of the initiative. The chapter concludes with an analysis of the initiative's strengths and weaknesses, and also provides a perspective on what could have been done differently.

How the Initiative Started

In 1993, a broad range of women's organisations, feminists and academics came together to prepare for the International Conference on Population and Development (ICPD), to be held in Cairo in 1994. Participants were concerned about the imposition of population control policies on poor women living in developing countries. Their main objective was to put women on the centre of the stage, as human beings with human rights. Cairo turned out to be the right place, at the right moment, for claiming a radical change in the predominant perspective. The Conference did not set a decrease in population as a goal. Rather, it achieved a substantial shift towards the advancement of reproductive rights for every human being. Furthermore, a more *humane* understanding of development goals and society's underlying gender inequities was reached (Espinosa, 1999: 27).

This initial collaboration among diverse Mexican groups turned into the Foro Nacional de Mujeres y Políticas de Población (Foro), a network that links together almost 80 women's organisations working in 17 out of the 32 states in the country. The main objective of the Foro is to ensure that the agreements reached and the benchmarks set at Cairo by 184 countries become a reality.

In 1999, when the first revision of the ICPD Programme of Action (PoA) was due, there was widespread concern among feminist organisations that the reproductive health perspective adopted in Cairo would be pushed back. It was believed that governments would argue that this holistic approach was too expensive to be consistently carried out. At the same time, the organisations suspected that the financial commitments of both governments and multilateral agencies had not been implemented. The PoA explicitly states that two-thirds of the resources allocated to 'human development' in developing countries should come from national sources. It states further that, in addition to the 0.7 per cent of Gross Domestic Product (GDP) for development assistance, 5,700 million dollars should be channelled from North to South.

Motivated by the need to know where Mexico as a nation stood in relation to ICPD's financial goals, a group of high-profile researchers of the Foro carried out an initial analysis of trends in federal programmes and spending regarding reproductive health. The study found that, between 1993 and 1996, federal expenditure in reproductive health dropped by 33 per cent in real terms, while government health expenditures in general dropped by an astounding 36 per cent. IMSS-Solidaridad, a nationwide health programme supporting Mexico's poorest people, was allocated only 3.8 per cent of the 1996 federal health budget to cover the needs of over 14 million people.

Furthermore, case studies of four states illustrated the narrow application of the concept of reproductive health. The research highlighted the inequities faced by different groups of women regarding birth control methods, maternal mortality and comprehensive attention to their health requirements. The analysis looked at diverse axes of discrimination stemming from class, ethnicity, age and the urban-rural split.

Simultaneously, a series of public finance workshops for women leaders was launched by Equidad de Género, Ciudadanía, Trabajo y Familia (Equidad), a feminist organisation operating within the nationwide network of the Foro. The path-breaking study of reproductive health expenditure, together with the opportunity of having public officials addressing questions about the federal budget, underscored the critical need for tools to advocate for a more gender-sensitive allocation of resources.

Meanwhile, pressure to integrate a gender perspective into public institutions and policy-making processes increased. The establishment of state and federal committees on gender and equity provided an opportunity for women to express their political views formally, and thus influence public policies. As a direct result of the creation of a gender desk within the Department of Social Development, a gender equity provision was established as part of the operational framework of anti-poverty programmes. This provision stated that every programme should allocate 50 percent of its resources to women.

The Focus on Anti-poverty Programmes: Building up a Joint Initiative

In 2000 Equidad and Fundar, a think tank mainly dedicated to applied budget research as a means of promoting democratisation, started a joint project on gender-sensitive budget analysis. The project operated at federal level as well as in four states. It began by training and collaborating with groups belonging to the Foro, a feminist political association called Diversa and the network Milenio Feminista (Milenio). The collaborative effort reached out to a broad audience, linking together two essential components: the solid technical skills of a research centre and the broad advocacy experience of feminist organisations and networks. The initiative was primarily supported by the Ford Foundation, as well as by Population Action International and General Services.

During its first year, this collaborative initiative focused on 21 government-funded anti-poverty programmes. Two crucial issues were examined: First, the initiative looked at whether and how neutrally framed programmes acknowledged and addressed the limits and structural difficulties faced by women. Second, it examined whether women's immediate needs were being covered and their capacities built.

At state level, analysis centred on two specific efforts of the anti-poverty strategy. The first was a programme of basic health extension to communities with no formal access to health services (Programa de Ampliación de Cobertura, PAC). The second was the anti-poverty programme of the federal government, Programa de Educación, Salud y Alimentación (PROGRESA). PROGRESA has been considered to be the most comprehensive and important approach to poverty reduction on the part of the Mexican government, encompassing health, education and nutrition. PAC operated under a five-year loan from the World Bank, while PROGRESA is funded directly by government.

The initiative's focus on the poorest and most marginalised sectors of the Mexican population was particularly important given the socio-economic context. The economic crises of the 1980s led the Government to implement several economic stabilisation and structural adjustment programmes. The currency was devalued, fiscal austerity was imposed and public expenditure as a percentage of GDP was steadily reduced. These measures had a direct impact on society, and especially on women living in near poverty conditions. Real wages fell and the resources available to meet basic needs diminished. As a result of shrinking employment opportunities and negative wage growth, extreme poverty affected 27 million people in 1999 according to official data, and twice as many according to independent researchers (Boltvinik, 2000: 12).

87

Research (Vinay et al, 2001) also found that half of all the anti-poverty programmes registered cutbacks from 2000 to 2001. These cutbacks affected nutrition, basic housing, temporary employment and community services. Among the 21 programmes analysed in more detail, only four were specifically targeting women, while six made an explicit reference to a gender perspective in their guidelines. Of these six, half registered cutbacks. The actual amount of money being spent on women by each of the programmes was difficult to estimate due to the lack of gender-disaggregated information. Both PROGRESA and PAC relied for their operation on the extension of women's traditional roles in nutrition, health and reproduction, implying additional and unpaid work.

Research carried out at sub-national level (Aguilar, forthcoming; Freyermuth, forthcoming) pointed to a limited vision regarding women's health needs. Generally speaking, the concept of comprehensive health services and recognition of gender inequities were absent. The criteria used to select the diseases to be addressed by the programme failed to establish clearly the different epidemiological situation of women and men. Although PAC included, among its thirteen actions, three which are specifically oriented towards women, the omission of gender criteria resulted in an inefficient assignment of resources. Furthermore, the specific actions to address women's health problems were not implemented with a gender perspective.

The Change in Government: New spaces for participation and a focus on health

In July 2000 a historic change reshaped the political landscape of Mexico. After over 70 years of one-party rule by the Partido Revolucionario Institucional (PRI), the centre-right Partido Acción Nacional (PAN) won the federal election. As in transition processes elsewhere, it was recognised that this change would open major windows of opportunity to influence the new government's agenda. Nevertheless, the feminist movement also expressed concern about the possible promotion of a conservative agenda. The time frame for defining spaces of participation and making full use of them in order to have an input into the policies of the coming years was crucial.

A forum on gender and health

The initial research of Foro, and the activities carried out regarding targeted expenditures for women and anti-poverty programmes by Equidad and Fundar, gave the gender budget initiative the leverage needed to push the topic of gender-sensitive spending further. At the beginning of 2001 discussions began among the different groups involved in the gender budget initiative and UNIFEM, in order to foster a concrete space for addressing health policies. The World Health Organization (WHO), the Pan American Health Organization (PAHO), the United Nations Population Fund (UNFPA) and the Department of Health were part of the effort.

In an environment of openness and consultation, a three-day forum was officially endorsed by the Department of Health. The main purpose was to generate proposals to be fed into the development of the six-year sectoral programme of the Department. The forum had an ambitious agenda, covering a broad variety of topics dealing with the complete life cycle of women. It was also the space for the announcement of a new government programme, 'Woman and Health', aimed at mainstreaming gender throughout the sector.

Plenary sessions addressing general concerns regarding gender and health were presided over by the Minister of Health, with the participation of national and international experts. These sessions set the tone for multidisciplinary working groups that focused on particular problems in a collaborative and interdisciplinary way. Each session presented a three-fold perspective: that of governmental agencies, research or academic institutions and civil society.

The closing plenary of the forum was used to introduce a new element into discussion, namely the need to advance towards a gender-sensitive health budget. The presentation in this session highlighted the difficulties faced by Foro's initial research as a result of the lack of appropriate budgetary information and gender-disaggregated data. The impossible task of identifying the budgetary dimensions of diverse components within specific programmes or units, as well as their beneficiaries, was underscored. Further complications were mentioned, such as the difficulties of linking up budget allocations and assessments, impact evaluation and, last but not least, efficiency (Hofbauer, 2001).

Input into the National Health Programme and further steps

As a result of the forum, dozens of specific proposals regarding all the topics covered by the plenary and working sessions were personally handed to the Minister of Health in order to be fed into the National Health Programme. Legislative reform, programme design and evaluation, research and training activities, communication, gender-sensitive budgets and the need for comprehensive services – including mental health, addictions and violence – were highlighted.

These actions, the broad coalitions behind them, the seriousness of the proposals and the commitment of the Department of Health made it possible to lay the initial ground for a constructive and collaborative relationship. Furthermore, the creation of a technical committee within the Woman and Health programme, aimed at consolidating a formal space of interaction, collaboration and follow-up of these proposals, was suggested and welcomed. The committee was composed of a diversity of actors, in order to contribute to the aim of mainstreaming gender into the whole array of activities to be undertaken by the Department. Working groups were defined and a gender-sensitive budget group was established. The idea of gender-sensitive budgets had thus reached the policy agenda and achieved formal endorsement.

A Glance inside the Process: The Difference between Knowing the Path and Walking the Path

Initial steps

As part of the activities carried out with the Woman and Health programme, a review of the programmatic structure of the whole Department of Health was undertaken. The review sought concrete ways to make initial steps towards the introduction of gender criteria into its main framework. Despite taking place during the new administration's first stage of budget formulation, specific proposals to change the programmatic structure were not put forward. Due to both the inexperience of the administration and lack of time, programme and budget officers stuck strictly to 'proved and tested' formats.

Simultaneously and during the rest of 2001, the Mexican gender budget initiative developed different approaches in order to reach out to government departments, committees in Congress, parts of the national women's machinery, media and other organisations of civil society. At the national level, several training and sensitisation workshops were conducted, and a formal event in Congress was launched by Equidad and a broad coalition of NGOs calling for "more equitable spending". Attention was thus increasingly drawn to the topic.

These activities were further strengthened and complemented by work at the sub-national level. The team in Chiapas engaged their own newly-elected provincial government. They ran workshops for public officials and the state-based institute for women, and submitted the results of their analysis to government departments. Their long-standing experience on health issues, particularly maternal mortality, and their solid technical analysis opened up spaces for dialogue and participation.

The team working in Queretaro inserted its budget research and activities into the broader campaign 'Women's Eyes on the World Bank', which operated in several states of the country. As a result, they also engaged directly with state and federal structures, particularly those responsible for implementing the health extension package (PAC). The friendly relations established with the Department of Health, the results of their research, and the political work regarding the inclusion of gender-sensitive budgets in the agenda all fostered further opportunities for dialogue and exchange.

A Second Step: A workshop for public officials

During the last four months of 2001, the Woman and Health programme, along with the groups involved in the gender budget initiative, started planning a workshop. The target audience was public officials implementing health extension programmes for the poorest sectors of society. Building on previous experiences, the workshop addressed general issues regarding gender, with the aim of fostering an understanding of the socially constructed differences between men and women. In order to illustrate the differentiated impact of neutrally defined programmes on women and men – and on different groups of women and men – the group chose to focus on two out of 13 components of the basic health package, namely diabetes mellitus and family planning. This workshop was the first formal attempt to bring officials involved in planning, budgeting and programme design of the Department of Health into a workshop to discuss gender-sensitive budgets.

The working session illustrated the differences in design, prioritisation and allocation of resources resulting from a gender focus. The practical exercises carried out were based on official information, covering the following:

◆ the epidemiological information that the Department of Health itself generates,

◆ the normative frameworks and procedures that regulate governmental actions regarding family planning and diabetes mellitus,

◆ the socio-demographic profile of a specific state,

◆ the programmatic components of PAC and its budgetary allocations.

As a result of a set of questions answered during the day, it became evident that in order to address the specific needs of women and men consistently, additional criteria had to be incorporated and resources allocated accordingly. Furthermore, it became clear that, in order to foster gender-sensitive budget allocations, a similar process had to be undertaken by every single unit of the Department. This realisation provided a perspective on the time frame within which the concept of gender-sensitive budgets moves ahead.

Despite again working during the formulation stage of the budget process, major changes could still not be expected. Willingness, commitment and official endorsement granted the opportunity of working in that stage, but capacities to develop a comprehensive and far-reaching process aimed at engendering the budget are just starting to be in place.

An initial guide on gender-sensitive budgets for the Department of Health

Building up gender-sensitive budget literacy among public officials, in a wide-ranging and consistent fashion, is a much-needed step in order to turn the expressed commitment and openness of the Department of Health into actual results. The challenge is two-fold. On the one hand it means repeatedly illustrating the need and the logic behind gender-sensitive programmatic design and allocation of resources. This, in itself, is a long road. On the other hand, the Mexican gender budget initiative itself has to make a conceptual leap from gender budget analysis to gender-sensitive budget formulation. Despite the initiative not being responsible for actually drawing up the budget, and thus not knowing internal technicalities, the urgent need to have clear suggestions on how to actually engender the budget keeps increasing.

It was recognised that without clearly explaining what gender-sensitive budgets are about, and what their development implies, progress would be limited to a few targeted expenditures. It was therefore decided that the most appropriate step was to aim at wide-ranging sensitisation. As a result, the case studies discussed in the workshop, as well as other documents on gender-sensitive budgets, were put together in a handbook published by the Department of Health. This handbook was distributed to every head of a directorate, state-based department or institute, and local-level health jurisdiction during mid-2002.

The message of the handbook is clear and simple, namely that budgets and programmes are not neutral, gender and sex are not the same, and that in order to address the needs of women and men and different groups of women and men, the socially constructed differences and opportunities have to be acknowledged. Equity, transparency, accountability, efficiency and effectiveness are explained as some of the positive by-products of a gender-sensitive resource allocation. Finally, the questions that guided the workshop with Department of Health officials, and the conclusions reached for each case, are discussed so as to suggest an approach to what has to be done in order to achieve these ends.

The handbook will be the first in a series to be published throughout the administration. The Department of Health will assist in engaging at least some units into supported processes in order to start the next planning phase with a gender perspective and analysis already in place. In the words of the Minister of Health, "the Ministry is committed to developing a methodology for the gender-sensitive formulation of the sectoral budgets… in order to progressively achieve their institutionalisation towards the end of the current administration" (quoted in Hofbauer et al, 2002: 15).

Additional Activities of the Gender Budget Initiative

On a parallel path to the one being walked with the Department of Health, the Mexican gender budget initiative has been growing and diversifying. After two years of a joint, collaborative project aimed at building up budget literacy and analytical capacity among the groups in the initiative, several diverse projects have evolved. Interest continues to grow, and opportunities continue to arise.

93

Maternal mortality

One of the projects currently being carried out by Fundar, together with two state-based groups of Foro and Equidad, aims at evaluating the impact of the budget's resource allocation in the reduction of maternal mortality. Although the ratio of maternal mortality in Mexico reflects a downward tendency (from 5.4 per 10,000 live births in 1990 to 4.9 per 10,000 live births in 1999), this achievement still places the country at a considerable distance from the targets agreed on in Cairo. According to the official report of the Department of Health, 68.3 per cent of maternal deaths occur among the population without social security assistance. As such, maternal mortality is closely related to lack of access to health care and emergency services.

This project brings the state of Oaxaca into the initiative, and continues the work in Chiapas. These two states have the highest maternal mortality rates in the country. The project builds on research, fieldwork regarding access to, and quality and availability of, the needed services, as well as on the scope of actions being implemented.

Decentralisation

The project 'Participatory Citizenship and Government Accountability for Gender-Sensitive Public Spending' focuses on accountability and, above all, on building a participatory citizenship capable of playing an active role in advocacy and monitoring the distribution of budget resources. The project is carried out by Equidad, with three teams working at state level in Chiapas, Oaxaca and the Federal District. Fundar is involved on the technical side.

Participants in both Chiapas and the Federal District are analysing decentralised resources for health services, while the initiative in Oaxaca aims at building the role of women in decision-making processes regarding resource allocation of decentralised anti-poverty funds at municipal level.

The main objective of the decentralisation project is to contribute to increasing gender-sensitive public spending and achieving transparency of public budgets. It hopes to do this by advocating for government accountability and proposing concrete changes in public policies at federal and state levels.

National and sub-national women's machineries

During 2001 the gender budget initiative began interacting with national and sub-national women's machineries. Proposals to include gender-sensitive budgets in the National Pro-Equity Programme, which structures the activities of the national women's machinery, were presented at a nation-wide consultation carried out by the government. Training and presentations were given in several states throughout the country.

With the support of the United Nations Development Programme (UNDP), an initial two-day workshop for the National Women's Institute was undertaken at the beginning of 2002. Subsequently, a formal project of collaboration between the Institute, Fundar and Equidad has started. The main objective is to identify concrete ways in which the Institute can use its mandate of mainstreaming gender into all sectors of government in order to promote gender-sensitive budgets.

Following the example of the process with the Department of Health, training and analysis of programmatic criteria will be undertaken in other sectors. Simultaneously, an eight-hour session on gender-sensitive budgets has been included in a comprehensive training course on gender and public policies. This training course is attended primarily by officials of the state-based women's machineries and other departments.

Lessons Learned and Pending Challenges

Writing this chapter has meant reflecting on the different aspects that have given the Mexican gender budget initiative its current shape. Sitting down and taking notes of the processes in which we are engaged on a daily basis is unfortunately something most advocates forget to do under the continuous pressure of responding to immediate events. Such reflection is, however, crucial in order to identify those elements that give strength to what we are doing, as well as the ones that need to be further developed.

The first strength of our initiative lies in the collaboration among diverse actors with complementary skills. This is especially important given the initial location of the initiative in civil society. On one hand, the keen political vision and advocacy capacities of women's organisations, and their ability to open up processes through the legitimacy of broad-based nation-wide networks, has been a crucial

95

element. On the other hand, the development of solid research capacities, as well as of clear arguments based on that research, has been key to developing the ability to engage in technical arguments with those who are responsible for budgets. The combination of these two factors, pictured as the two legs of applied budget analysis, are probably the single most important strength of the Mexican initiative. Budget analysis is doomed to fail if it is restricted to academic documents which are detached from real concerns and thus fail to drive the actions of real people. Similarly, advocacy without solid information is unlikely to go far.

This initial strength is the basis of the initiative's ability to create awareness around the need for more equitable and gender-sensitive budgets. A second strength has been the ability to push the issues of gender-sensitive budgets and equitable spending onto the political agenda. The leverage the initiative has gained through sensitising diverse actors, who have carried the message further, is an important element.

The process of establishing opportunities for dialogue and even collaboration with the government has been partially a result of the change in the overall political landscape of the country. In this sense, the opportunities that arise when a government talks about far-reaching changes are invaluable when one is embarking on proposals that question what has been done before. Gender-sensitive budgets question predominant paradigms. These are often under revision, at least to some extent, when major changes in government occur.

The opportunities for collaboration, and the position in which the Mexican initiative finds itself currently, point to the success of its initial phases. They also point to a whole new array of challenges and unresolved questions. It is here that some of the major challenges for gender budget initiatives worldwide come into the picture. What has to be done once it really starts happening? What kind of capacities have to be developed in order to have the strengths needed – both in terms of skills and human resources – to turn the commitment and willingness of government agencies into concrete action?

Despite the involvement of broad-based networks, advocacy groups and grassroots organisations in some of the state-based projects, one of the challenges faced by the Mexican gender budget initiative is that participation is still very limited. Because of the technical skills required, it has been extremely difficult to create messages that empower women who are not engaged in the process so as to enhance the role they play within their environments.

Another challenge is the ability to make a process like the one the Mexican initiative has been following in health replicable in other sectors. Is it possible to develop the same leverage for education, labour and housing issues, for example? One perspective would make us believe that by opening up this process, getting fully engaged in it and achieving concrete results, the need for equitable and gender-sensitive spending will be 'modelled', and thus feasible to replicate. Another perspective points to the possibility that in order to develop the same leverage regarding other issues, a similar step-by-step, long-term process will have to be followed.

Lastly, the achievement of a certain level of awareness regarding the topic, as well as the commitment and willingness of particular sectors, points only to a halfway success, namely, highlighting an unfulfilled need. The other half involves actually implementing a gender-sensitive budget, through the development of strategies that might require a different combination of public awareness and technical capacities. In this sense, the differences between knowing the path and walking the path are still to be explored.

References

Aguilar P. (Forthcoming). *Report on State Activities*. Queretaro.

Boltvinik J. (2000). "El Error de Levy" in *La Jornada*, 25 February.

Espinosa G., L.P. Paredes and V. Rodríguez (1999). *Salud Sexual y Reproductiva en México: los Programas, los Procesos, los Recursos Financieros*, UAM Xochimilco, Mexico.

Freyermuth G. (Forthcoming). "Report on State Activities: Budget allocation to the health sector in the state of Chiapas."

Hofbauer H. (2001). "Presupuestos con enfoque de género: el caso de salud," seminario Género y Política de Salud, Mexico City, Mexico, 7–9 March.

_____, D. Sánchez and V. Zebadúa (2002). *Presupuestos sensibles al género: conceptos y elementos básicos*. Secretaría de Salud, Mexico.

Vinay C., H. Hofbauer, L. Pérez-Fragoso and C. Martínez (2001). *Mujeres y Pobreza: el presupuesto del gasto social focalizado visto desde la perspectiva de género*, Fundar-Equidad de Género, Mexico.

The Philippines: Getting smart with local budgets

Celia Flor and Andrea Lizares-Si

Table 8: Selected indicators for The Philippines

Indicator	Year	Number
Population	2002	79.5 million
% of population which is female	2002	49.6%
% of population which is urban		n/a
Gross domestic product (GDP) per capita (US$)	1999	3,805
Human development index (HDI)	1999	0.749
Gender development index (GDI)	1999	0.746
% of total budget funded by donors		n/a
% of national parliamentarians who are women	2001	Senate: 7.7% Congress: 16.75

Introduction

As in most third world countries, local governments in the Philippines are cash-strapped when it comes to government programmes and projects that are meaningful for women or for the cause of gender and development (GAD). To give more specific impetus to inclusion of GAD in budgeting, beginning in 1995 the General Appropriations Act which approves the national budget mandated that all national agencies set aside 5 per cent of their agency budgets for GAD. In 1998 local governments were likewise required to allocate 5 per cent of their total budgets for GAD. The intended purpose of this law was not to limit government spending for GAD to 5 per cent. Rather, the 5 per cent was meant to provide national agencies and local government units (LGUs) with a budget for programmes that would enhance the agency's capability for gender-sensitive planning and budgeting. The ultimate objective was to mainstream GAD in the remaining 95 per cent of the budget.

The law was clear, but its implementation was not. Over the years, some national agencies and LGUs charged salaries and benefits of women government employees, items such as ballroom dancing lessons, and the total budgets of LGU social services departments to the 5 per cent budget. For some, the GAD budget became the purse from which all kinds of unbudgeted grants and expenses could be paid. On the other hand, well-meaning national agencies and LGUs that tried to give life to the spirit of the act found the 5 per cent to be an additional burden on already insufficient resources. Meanwhile, non-government organisations (NGOs), especially those working for women, waited in frustration for policy and budget reforms that would mean funds for tangible GAD programmes and projects.

Development Through Active Women Networking Foundation (DAWN) was one of these NGOs. This chapter tells the story of our work to influence planning and budgeting in our LGU, the City of Bacolod. We also describe how examining our city's budget through a gender lens provided us with invaluable insight into the workings of LGUs in general, and our own local unit in particular. These learnings have been useful for our advocacy work and for the training we conduct to equip women for political involvement. The research also provided DAWN with the opportunity to work with key LGU personnel and to create a core group of GAD allies and advocates within the government unit.

The process of doing the research was not easy, but we managed to do it despite the fact that we are not professional researchers, nor are we accountants with a technical understanding of budgets. In fact, one of the team members "abhors" dwelling on budgets as she considers them too technical and limiting within the framework of government budgeting and accounting rules. By sharing our story, we hope to enable other women and development advocates to benefit from our experience. But first, a brief background on DAWN and our City of Bacolod.

DAWN foundation

DAWN is an NGO based on Negros island that was founded in 1990 primarily to promote gender sensitivity in both the public and private sectors, and to organise a network of women's organisations in the island's two provinces. DAWN has always believed in partnership with government. The opportunity for a strong working relationship with the City of Bacolod, capital of Negros Occidental, presented itself in 1992 when Luzviminda Valdez was elected our first female councillor.

By then, DAWN had earned the right to be recognised as the local expert not only on women's issues, but also on the national government's GAD programmes. In 1993, through the efforts of Valdez and DAWN, the Bacolod Consortium of Women's Organisations (BCWO) was founded to manage the Women's Centre, a crisis centre that would be built and operated with public funds on public land. DAWN was also able to obtain government funds to sustain activities celebrating Women's Month in March and the 16 Days of Activism Against Gender Violence in November-December.

Appreciation of how an NGO can influence public policy for the enhancement of women's status was bolstered in 1994 through training for potential GAD advocates in the province. The training on legislative advocacy for women's issues and the drafting and promotion of ordinances resulted in the formation of a group which researched, drafted and lobbied for the passage of an ordinance creating and providing funds for the Provincial Council for Women (PCW). The PCW has since then become a strong and active provincial network of GAD advocates who work closely with LGUs throughout the province. With DAWN as consultant, the PCW initiated gender mainstreaming efforts in these LGUs.

1995 was a particularly successful year for DAWN. After the inauguration of the Women's Centre in January, DAWN began its Women in Politics Project to take forward the advocacy for women's political participation. Executive Director Celia Flor agreed to run for the City Council, thus serving as guinea pig for the project and bringing GAD and other basic needs issues into the public forum. She won her seat, but unfortunately the administration which had been supportive of her and Valdez lost. This meant funds for the Women's Centre and city-wide awareness and advocacy activities were more difficult to obtain. Not to be stymied by a lack of budget resources, DAWN worked directly with government agencies that were already partners of the women's consortium, influencing and assisting them so that the thrust of their services would be more responsive to women's needs.

DAWN lacked clout within the top level of the political leadership during the six years from 1995 to 2001. However, it used the time to expand its influence in other directions and forge new alliances. Training on women in politics was conducted for women leaders from the province as well as grassroots women. Many of the latter now hold key positions in their villages and serve as a powerful mass base for initiatives where GAD and local budgets are concerned. Through the PCW, inroads were made into the provincial government of Negros Occidental and component cities and municipalities.

In 1998, DAWN's expertise in GAD was officially recognised when DAWN President (also BCWO President) Andrea Si was invited, along with Celia Flor, to participate in regional training on GAD planning and budgeting. Si was the city's only non-government participant in this training, which was organised by the Department of Interior and Local Government (DILG) for heads of selected LGU offices and agencies. A significant development of this partnership was an unwritten policy for DILG to ensure the 5 per cent GAD fund in the budgets of *barangays* (villages), and their submission of GAD entry plans before ratification by the City Council.

Bacolod City

Bacolod is a highly urbanised city that is the seat of government, commerce, education and cultural activities of Negros Occidental. In 1995, the National Statistics Office (NSO) reported that the city's population was 402,345. Of this, 196,601 were male and 205,744 female. 304,194 resided in the city's 20 rural or suburban *barangays* and 98,151 in the 41 urban *barangays*.

At the time the research was conducted, the city's Mayor was male, the Vice-Mayor was female, and three of the 14 councillors were female. The two gender advocates were in the opposition and the minority. There were more men than women among the rank and file and the temporary employees of the City Council. Women predominated at the second level (division chief, section chief, supervisor), but thinned out drastically at the highest level.

Beginning in 1998 the City Council passed resolutions requiring 5 per cent of the budget to be reserved by each department for GAD programmes and projects. Budgets were, however, approved even without the 5 per cent being set aside. The Council was generally uncooperative because the party in power perceived the leadership of gender advocacy to belong to the opposition. This is a perplexing example of a council ignoring its own policies, a not uncommon occurrence in local partisan politics. Fortunately, many government agency heads and key personnel were already GAD advocates or were at least receptive to integrating GAD in their agency programmes and projects, if only they knew how.

Aside from its officials and employees, the city can count on an active civil society led by 63 accredited NGOs and civic organisations. In 2000, 26 of these accredited organisations were represented in the City Development Council (CDC), a body composed of government and non-government representatives who formulate and propose the City's Development Plan and its accompanying Annual Investment Plan for the Mayor and the City Council to approve. Since the CDC is a local 'special body' created under the Local Government Code, this participation gives civil society a certain measure of influence in the planning and budgeting processes.

Gender Budget Advocacy and Budget Research

Beginning in 1997 DAWN's staff and trustees became involved, first as participants and later as trainers, in government and private sector seminars for GAD planning and budgeting. While we realised early on that members of civil society have a right to question how public funds are used and to intervene in policy making, planning, budgeting and evaluation, it was not until we conducted our gender budget research in 2000 that we studied in detail the local budgeting process and how it was actually practiced in the city.

Investigating the budget shed light on where public funds go. In particular, it showed how much goes for feeding the bureaucracy and how much for services and programmes that directly benefit the public, particularly women. For instance, after we conducted the research we were able to point out how our city government budgeted a measly P2 million for medicines for a constituency of about 450,000 people, while about 10 per cent of the budget was expended for the salaries of temporary government workers, many of whom had been hired to repay political debts. This amount was in addition to the budget of regular employees, which already amounted to 47 per cent (in 1999) and 59 per cent (in 2000) of the total budget, more than the government-prescribed ceiling of 45 per cent.

DAWN agreed to do the research, which was funded by The Asia Foundation (TAF), because we saw the study as an opportunity to document our decade-long advocacy efforts in GAD in Bacolod City and the province of Negros Occidental. It was an opportunity to use a gender lens to take a closer look at the city's budget, how this budget is appropriated, who decides, who benefits and what the bases are for appropriating.

We also saw that the project could open doors for us where influencing government planning and budgeting were concerned. This was important because, although DAWN's executive director was already a city councillor, under the Local Government Code of the Philippines budgets are proposed by the Chief Executive (our Mayor), and the city councillors' influence is limited to approving disapproving or reducing the proposed budget. Councillors do not have the power to add or change items. Through the case study we hoped to discover alternative ways to mainstream gender in the city's programmes and projects, even when a chief executive is gender blind or hostile to the proponents of GAD. We wanted to find out if and how the city used the 5 per cent GAD fund. We were also interested in discovering how the remaining 95 per cent was used.

Our objectives for doing the research were:

◆ To inquire into the utilisation of the 5% GAD budget for two fiscal years and to look into the impact of the 5% on the 95% budget as far as mainstreaming GAD is concerned;

◆ To provide the LGU of Bacolod City with recommendations on indicators, policies and mechanisms for increasing the gender responsiveness of the city's budget and for formulating and implementing a GAD plan.

◆ To pinpoint gaps in the local planning and budgeting process and identify areas where sectoral and civil society interventions would be beneficial.

Backstage of the research

Work on the research happened on two levels. The first level was with the funding agency, TAF, and the stakeholders in the three geographical areas identified as case studies. The latter included NGOs, the national government machinery and the LGUs. The second level of the work involved the gathering of information and the writing of the research report.

To prepare the stakeholders and guide us as the work proceeded, regular meetings and workshops were organised by TAF. The first meeting had all stakeholders agreeing on three points: (a) a common set of objectives for the compilation of gender budget case studies; (b) that, because of time constraints, our study would focus on the performance of three local government departments that are presumed to be front liners in GAD work; and (c) that we would adopt a uniform outline for our reports.

To help us reach agreement on the components necessary for the outline, our TAF facilitators, led by South African gender budget expert Debbie Budlender, conducted workshops that enabled us to determine what kind of information is necessary for anyone who wishes to participate in, influence or even just understand government planning and budgeting. We took part in games, structured learning exercises and role playing as practical tools for analysis, to understand how people in certain positions of power, with certain perspectives, sensitivities and agendas, make policy decisions which create programmes and decide how resources are utilised.

Since we were inexperienced at this kind of research, the outline which was agreed on during the workshop served as an indispensable step-by-step guide for the information that we had to gather and the order in which this was to be put together. This outline was as follows:

◆ Background of the NGO conducting the research or whose involvement with the local government is part of the GAD budget story of that local government. This was our chance to tell the story of DAWN Foundation;

◆ Information on our city and the LGU, including population, economy, critical issues for women and key gender concerns, decision-making and policies;

◆ The planning and budgeting process of the local government, both as mandated by official policy and as happens in practice;

◆ Budget implementation and monitoring, including both revenue and expenditure, and the GAD budget;

◆ GAD in three selected departments, including a description of functions, objectives, activities, total budget and GAD budget; and

◆ Lessons and recommendations for NGOs and civil society and for government.

Equipped with the outline and renewed motivation, we returned to our cities and began the work of data gathering and analysis. Assistance and supervision from TAF continued during this period. After several months in the field, we met again to evaluate our own work and that of the other teams and to learn from each other. Data gathering and the preparation of the research report thus became a 'learn by doing' team exercise that made the work easier and even fun. While the subject of gender, GAD and GAD budgeting is quite complex, broad and encompassing, the agreed outline and continuing 'critique-ing' workshops helped redirect researchers back to the objectives. It thus reduced the temptation to stray as data gathering revealed unexpected 'discoveries' or interesting sidelights.

Data gathering

One of the most important decisions we made was the decision to do the research ourselves although, as mentioned earlier, we are not professional researchers, accountants or budget experts. Knowing our limitations, we planned to get our work done by drawing our key informants from the local government into a partnership with us.

We began with a letter informing the Mayor that, in recognition of Bacolod's pioneering work in GAD, the prestigious Asia Foundation had selected the city from among all the cities and municipalities in the country to be one of three sites for the gender budget research. We then requested him to direct the officials involved in planning and budgeting, as well as the key people in the departments we had selected, to cooperate with us so as to facilitate the research. Although Celia Flor and her closest political ally Luzviminda Valdez, who at the time of the research was Vice-Mayor and a very vocal opponent of the Mayor, were tagged as political opposition, we were given the endorsement that we needed.

Seeking the Mayor's endorsement was our way of making him a strategic partner in the research. It allowed him the opportunity to 'own' the programme and project the image of being supportive of GAD mainstreaming, which is mandated by law and popular with civil society and women. The offer was also difficult to refuse as women constitute a large segment of his voting constituency.

The next step was to meet with our key informants among the government executives. We began by acknowledging their expertise as government executives, an expertise that they were often unable to use because of politics or the inflexibility of government procedures. We said we had worked with them enough in the past to appreciate their good intentions and share in their frustrations. We presented ourselves as doing the research project to help them and other government planners to understand and implement the mandatory 5 per cent gender budget more effectively. In exchange for information, we would teach them what we knew about gender issues and GAD plans. Together we would look at the budget to determine how much of it is actually being used for programmes and services that respond to the needs of the communities government is supposed to serve. Together we would discover how our government could better serve these people.

After this orientation on the project, we confessed our limitations and welcomed their readiness to provide us with information as well as refer us to other sources. We proceeded with an assessment of their needs. Through a participatory process, we made plans for gender sensitivity training, a seminar on gender issues and another on GAD planning and budgeting. Of course, the benefit of these trainings did not end with the research project.

Information was obtained from different sources and through different means. Through focus group discussions and individual interviews, we heard from our key informants about how the actual process of planning and budgeting compared with the process as mandated in government codes and manuals. Before our research report was finalised, we presented the draft to the key informants as a group and asked them to validate our findings. We were never ashamed to ask, and our partners never faltered in their eagerness to help.

We also held a focus group discussion with civil society leaders to elicit information and feedback on their participation in the CDC. They identified facilitating and hindering factors to meaningful participation and shared their thoughts on how civil society participation could be strengthened to give more meaning to the law.

Village heads, chairpersons of the village committee for women and children, and GAD focal points provided data for our report on the village GAD budgets. They also shared with us their perceptions of the impact of government projects on the villages, especially on the lives of women and children.

For more details on our selected departments, the research team interviewed personnel involved in the department's planning process and those providing direct services. The annual accomplishment reports of the departments were also used as a source of valuable data, not only about the department's performance but also on general statistics and issues.

In addition, we looked at the city development plan, the annual investment plan, a proposed land use plan, the Mayor's annual report on the city, and government publications on the mandated procedure for planning and budgeting in local governments. We did not examine them in depth but knew that at least we had to be familiar with their purpose and the information they contain.

Last, but definitely not least, we studied the thick print-outs of the proposed and approved budgets of the two years which were the periods covered by our research.

Making sense of the budget documents

A neophyte researcher is likely to take one look at the thick budget volumes and decide that nothing inside will ever make sense. However, it is impossible to do budget research if one does not learn to understand the budget as it is presented. It is helpful to remember that budgets are made to be considered by elected chief executives and local legislators who cannot be assumed to be literate about budgets either. While the document appears daunting, it is easier, as with any book, when one starts with the table of contents and goes through the volume part by part.

In the Philippines, all LGUs have more or less the same content for their budget books:

◆ The chief executive's budget message which outlines their main programme of government, their vision, and how these will be carried out through programme and budget priorities. This section often includes helpful charts, graphs and other information.

◆ There follow a number of statements and summaries such as statements of income and expenditure. These give an idea of who funds government operations, whether it is the landowners, the traders, the industrialists, the ordinary working people or the national government. This section includes summaries of appropriations that show how much each department or office gets for personal services, maintenance and other operating expenses (MOOE), capital outlay and non-office expenditures.

◆ The third section presents the budget for each department, beginning with the city mayor's office. Every presentation begins with a page containing the functional statement and general objectives of the department or office. This provides a general idea of what the people in the department think their work is about. It also reveals whether they considered GAD when making their plans and their budget.

◆ The last section contains a list of names of personnel per department, with information such as positions and salaries. This is not of much interest unless you wish to know how much a certain person earns, though low salaries do help to explain why there is graft and corruption in government.

The budget documents show figures for three years – the previous two years and the year of the budget. In most cases, the increase from year to year is a more or less fixed percentage. Where budget items disappear, or where there are large deviations in particular items from year to year, these are signposts for the researcher to ask why this happened.

Writing the research report

The outline agreed on in the workshops was a guide. It was not meant to be an inflexible master. For example, when we began gathering data, one of the first things we learned was that most departments did not have a 5 per cent GAD budget. Instead of just saying, "no GAD budget, end of story", we went on its trail. We examined how departments and offices incorporated GAD-related project activities or activities that address issues critical for women into the statements of their ordinary functions, objectives, and project activities. We found out that our selected departments had very little money for special projects because the bulk was allocated for salaries and operating expenses. However, some still managed to have GAD-related projects through funding from outside sources and through using the time-honoured volunteer labour and contributions of women.

As we worked, we became increasingly puzzled by how much was being poured into the government bureaucracy and how little was coming through by way of programmes and services. When we looked where the money went, we discovered that the City Mayor's Office controlled one-third of the total budget. It was from our investigation of this bloated budget that we learned many interesting things about how public funds can be mismanaged and lost.

Although, as long time GAD advocates, we were unhappy with what we had found out about our city's GAD budget, we were pleased to be able to discover through our research the more or less successful implementation of the 5 per cent GAD budget policy in our *barangays*, the smallest political unit of the city.

Our Findings

Researchers working with other cities and municipalities will make discoveries that are very different from ours. We present a few of our findings here to give an idea of the kind of information we thought important for our purpose. We focus on what we reported about budget implementation and monitoring, and about the Department of Social Services and Development (DSSD).

Revenues

The city's estimated total revenue according to the executive budget was P503.6 million in 1999 and P564 million in 2000. These amounts do not include contributions received from the Philippine Amusements and Gaming Corporation, programme grants from foreign funders, congressional funds which come via the city's congressperson, financial support from national agencies for devolved agencies, donations, and others. The budgeted revenue also does not include the *barangays'* share of the internal revenue allotment (IRA), which is channelled through the city for distribution to the *barangays*.

The city's share of the IRA is the largest single item of revenue. The IRA is the allocation of the LGU from the national taxes collected by the Bureau of Internal Revenue. It is apportioned to provinces, cities, municipalities and *barangays* according to a sharing scheme provided by the Local Government Code. In 1999, 56 per cent of budgeted revenue came from the IRA. This increased to 57 per cent in 2000. Other major sources of income were municipal business taxes (13–14%) and real property taxes (8–10%).

Expenses

The city's total expense budget was P503,600 for 1999 and P558,697 for 2000. The following table shows how the budget was divided in the two years.

Table 9: Bacolod budget, 1999 and 2000

Category	1999	% of total	2000	% of total
General services	239,106,669	47%	327,901,528	59%
Social services	135,564,770	27%	110,668,277	20%
Economic development	128,928,561	26%	120,127,312	21%
Total	503,600,000	100%	558,697,117	100%

The decrease of 25 million for social services and 8.8 million for economic development was caused mainly by the transfer of P33 million in salaries for temporary employees from the budgets of departments under these sectors to the mayor's office, which falls under general services. The bulk of the increase in the budget for general services also went to the mayor's office.

Every department's budget is broken down into personal services (salaries and employee benefits), MOOE, capital outlay and non-office expenditures. In 2000, 52 per cent of the general services budget, 72 per cent of social services and 40 per cent of economic development went for salaries and employee benefits. The percentage allocated for MOOE was 18 per cent, 11 per cent and 12 per cent respectively.

The 5 per cent GAD budget

Instead of allocating 5 per cent of the total budget for GAD, this percentage was based only on the budget for MOOE. In the year 2000, the total MOOE of all offices and departments came to P84,916,808, or 15 per cent of the total budget. The unwritten policy that based the 5 per cent GAD fund on the MOOE meant that only P4,245,840 was available for GAD-specific projects in 2000.

According to the City Budget Office, there was, in fact, much more for GAD-related programmes than the 5 per cent of the MOOE. The Office claimed that the city allocated more than 54 million in each of the two years for various programmes and projects which, in their understanding, were GAD-related. These would amount to more than 10 per cent of the total expense budget. However, the list provided by the budget officer included items that are difficult to justify as GAD-related. Among these are P5 million for a tax collection and information drive, almost P2.4 million for war veterans' welfare and development, P11 m for the public employment services fund,

P500,000 for Boy Scouts (versus P250,000 for Girl Scouts) and P3m for a sports development project. The last-named is particularly questionable as the city has no sports programme for women.

Even without a GAD plan, the city spends substantial amounts on programmes which address gender. However, the GAD budget is meant to be the GAD plan translated into the peso and centavo requirements for its implementation. We cannot therefore assign any expense item as part of the 5 per cent GAD budget unless there is a GAD plan and we see how this expense item fits into it.

Notwithstanding the absence of a GAD plan and budget items which are specifically identified as chargeable to the 5 per cent GAD fund, we observed the following from the department budgets and the accompanying introductory statements outlining functions, objectives and project activities:

◆ Some departments have statements of function, objectives and/or description of project activities that are GAD-related or have to do with issues identified as critical to women.

◆ GAD-related objectives and project activities of a department do not necessarily have an identifiable budget allocation. When the project activities are part of the ordinary operations of the department or office, the expense for the activity is included in the department's budget for personal services and for MOOE. In several cases, departments also included plans for project activities to be managed by the department's personnel, but with project funds and materials from the national government or from sources other than the local government.

◆ There is a noteworthy absence of GAD in the introductory statements of some key departments. Among the offices which should have GAD in their introductory statements are the following:

◇ Departments or offices responsible for data gathering and profiling – these could write into their office objectives the collection of sex-disaggregated data.

◇ Human Resource Management Services is well placed to include GAD-related awareness and capability building training for personnel. However, although this had GAD-related activities for 1999 and 2000, the introductory statements did not mention GAD.

◇ Bacolod Police Command is funded by the national government but received a budget of over P6 million from the city. The statement of objectives as reflected in the 2000 budget mentions intensifying the campaign against drug abuse but says nothing about violence against women. This despite the fact that the Bacolod Police Women's Desk is among the best in the country.

Interviews with heads of the DSSD, Health, Housing and other departments revealed a number of points which were important for our understanding of the budget documents.

The officials told us that the budgets for personal services and MOOE are generally fixed. The departments can do little to change them because items for spending in these areas are more or less stable from year to year. Department planning therefore mostly has to do with the identification of programmes and projects, the budget for which is categorised as 'non-office expenditures'.

Further, programmes and projects identified by departments or managed by them are not necessarily funded from their budget allocations. A total of P68,426,000, or 64 per cent of the total of P107,516,000 for non-office expenditures in 2000, was appropriated for the Mayor's Office, which then passed on funds to the departments. Social Services, Health and Housing also said that funds for certain programmes and projects might come from the non-office expenditure budget of a different department, or from other sources such as national agencies, congressional funds and grants.

Implementation and monitoring

Programmes and projects proposed by the various departments and eventually approved as part of their budgets are not automatically ready for implementation. Before the appropriation for a specific budgeted programme or project can be released, the department concerned has to submit its implementation plan or work programme.

After the work programme is approved by the mayor, the department prepares the necessary supporting documents and submits these to the City Treasurer for payment. Department heads who participated in the focus group discussion informed DAWN that they have had work programmes approved by the mayor but nevertheless not implemented because the city supposedly did not have funds available. This is disturbing because the work programmes are based on programmes and projects which are already part of the approved budget. According to some department heads, the lack of funds occurs when budget items are reverted to the general fund by the Budget Office without consulting the department head concerned.

The Local Government Code requires local governments to have project monitoring teams for monitoring project implementation. No such monitoring team functioned in 1999 and 2000 in Bacolod.

Department of Social Services and Development (DSSD)

This department is responsible for providing basic social welfare and development programmes and services; orientation and technical assistance to city officials and agencies on social welfare programmes; promoting individual and community welfare programmes and services; and recommending city and *barangay* ordinances for the protection and rehabilitation of groups with special needs. It has welfare programmes for families and communities; women, children and youth; the disabled and elderly and other disadvantaged groups and relief and rehabilitation programmes for distressed communities and sectors.

The regular work complement of the DSSD as of 30 June 2000 was 62 women and 7 men. The department head, three division heads, and three supervisory welfare officers were female, as were all the social workers and day care workers. Except for the day care workers, all the women had attended gender sensitivity training.

DSSD's budget

While the DSSD annually prepares budgets for its various programmes for vulnerable sectors, as a rule what is consolidated by the Budget Office and subsequently approved by the City Council provides only for personal services and MOOE. Personal services had a budget of close to P14 million in 1999 and about P 13 million in 2000. The reduction in 2000 was mainly due to the transfer of the salaries for temporary employees to the budget for the mayor's office.

The 2000 budget for non-officer expenditure amounted to about P8.5 million. This was divided as follows: 39 per cent for a nutrition programme; 28 per cent for veterans' welfare and development; 25 per cent for grants to private, non-government institutions such as orphanages, community hospitals or lying-in clinics and rehabilitation centres; 2 per cent for the City Drug Abuse Prevention Council; 2 per cent for the Reception, Diagnostic, Placement Centre; and less than 1 per cent each for the women's crisis centre and for a child-minding centre.

Because it does not receive sufficient programme funds from the city, the department is dependent on supplies and materials from the national government. It also has to resort to referrals and community-based resource generation for its other needs. For instance, in the programme for children, the DSSD pays an honorarium of P3,000 per month to each of 22 day care workers who teach pre-schoolers. These workers, all women, are at work from 8 am to 5 pm but are paid less than the P200 daily wage paid to temporary employees. Other expenses for the needs and activities of the children are either provided by the parents or funded through solicitations from private individuals, local government officials and civic clubs or service organisations. DSSD 's estimated monetary valuation of the funds and other resources which supported its programmes from January to June 2000 amounted to about P4.2 million. P3.2 of that total came from foreign funds coursed through the DILG for the Food for Work Programme and Educational Assistance. Only about P207,000 (less than 5%) of the P4.2 was used for programmes classified as 'women's welfare'. These included livelihood programmes, practical skills development, medical assistance, financial assistance, transportation, gender-sensitivity training and violence against women.

DSSD's GAD fund

Unlike some other departments, the DSSD does allocate 5 per cent of its MOOE for GAD. The project proposal for the department's GAD is usually prepared by the supervisor in charge of the women's programme. The programme of works is approved by the mayor and submitted to the budget office in February or March. However, projects are often implemented towards the second half of the year.

In 1999, DSSD allocated P98,000 for GAD but spent only P48,000 of the budgeted amount. It was informed by the budget office towards the last quarter of the year that the remaining GAD fund had reverted to the general fund and already allocated for expenses included in supplemental budgets. The P48,000 which the department received was used to subsidise the registration fees of DSSD social workers who attended the Philippine Association of Social Workers Convention in Bacolod City, and for other capacity building of staff. According to

DSSD, the registration fees were charged to the GAD fund because the convention was useful for updating the social workers on the current trends and issues confronting social work, and it enhanced their skills as service providers.

In 2000 DSSD's GAD fund included an allocation of P31,700 for a single person to attend a short training programme in Australia. Given that other programmes were not implemented due to lack of funds, and the fact that the Women's Centre received a maximum of P75,000 per year, this amount seems excessive.

Conclusion

Achievements to date

DAWN originally had some misgivings about conducting the research. Firstly, we were concerned that it would be perceived as a partisan political tool of the opposition to critique government. Secondly, we did not feel that the DAWN team had the necessary expertise. The organisation agreed to do the research so as to strengthen our ability to influence public policy within the local government context. Through its involvement in the initiative, DAWN has recognised that budgets, budget processes and the links to policy formulation and development planning are strategic to our goal of GAD mainstreaming not only in Bacolod City but in the whole province of Negros Occidental.

Prior to this initiative DAWN had made important inroads in respect of GAD mainstreaming advocacy with local governments through our various programmes on governance and women electoral politics. Studying local budgets did not seem a particularly palatable activity because of its 'boring', technical aspects. However, we recognised that budgets are an essential resource if government is to perform. They are also a route through which the constituency can make the LGU accountable in tangible terms. These realisations gave us a more positive outlook on budgets and the study.

The process of the research built our capacity and made us more confident in our advocacy work. We now know where to look for information, how to infer the implications of such information for the LGU's development plans and policies and GAD mainstreaming efforts, and when to suggest policy changes. All this new knowledge is significant for NGOs and advocates who want to do serious work on budget advocacy.

The research revealed that most, if not all, departments were concerned only with their own functions, programmes and plans and corresponding budget proposals, perhaps because they had not been given a chance to see their part in the big picture. There was no appreciation or conscious effort to look at the interconnectedness of one department's budget to the others' programmes and budget, or to the city's overall programmes and plans. Further, departments make their budgets from year to year and then wait for the budget office to slash them arbitrarily and without consultation. It had not occurred to many that, as major stakeholders within the bureaucracy, departments can and should have a say in the changes in their budgets. The research assisted them in seeing the whole, rather than simply the parts with which they are directly concerned.

Moving forward

Since doing the research, DAWN has moved forward with its work on GAD mainstreaming. In particular, it replicated the research in eleven component cities of the province of Negros Occidental, with additional funding support from The Asia Foundation. The focus group discussions among the cities' local finance committees, members of the council and some chief executives became an entry point for these local government units to consider seriously implementation of the GAD budget policy and GAD planning in their respective bureaucracies and constituencies. The provincial government has since sought the assistance of DAWN in formulating the province's GAD plan and budget.

In Bacolod City, DAWN is now coordinating GAD planning in preparation for budget year 2003. The expected output is the city's first GAD Plan, which will become part of the City Land Use and Development Plan. The City GAD focal point is responsible for the GAD planning. The Focal Point is a council composed of department heads and GAD champions from key departments and agencies, both public and private. The structure was created by an executive order issued by now city Mayor Luzviminda Valdez, and DAWN President Andrea Si sits in the Focal Point in her capacity as City Administrator.

Rwanda: Translating government commitments into action

Ngone Diop-Tine

Table 10: Selected Indicators for Rwanda

Indicator	Year	Number
Population	2001	7,979,930
% of population which is female	2001	54
% of population which is urban		
Gross Domestic Product (GDP) per capita (US$)	2001	885
Human Development Index (HDI)	2001	0.395
Gender Development Index (GDI)	2001	0.391
% of total budget funded by donors	2001	65%
% of national parliamentarians who are women	2002	17

Introduction

This chapter aims at sharing the experience of Rwanda in engendering the budget. As the initiative is ongoing, the chapter focuses mainly on what has been done so far, the strategies used, the strengths and weaknesses and the challenges. However, the chapter also briefly outlines future plans.

Table 10 highlights the main features of Rwanda's socio-economic and political context. Like many African countries, Rwanda's society is patriarchal and characterised by marked gender inequalities. Traditional gender imbalances were exacerbated by the 1994 genocide.

The population of Rwanda is estimated at 7,979,930 people, of whom 54 per cent are female. Women also head 34 per cent of households. Yet the 2000 Households Living Conditions and Core Welfare Indicators Questionnaire Survey found that women have limited access to social and economic services compared to men. For example, women's literacy rate is estimated at 47.8 per cent compared to 58.1 per cent for men. Women constitute more than 80 per cent of farmers, but have limited access to, and control over, assets including land, pesticides, seeds, markets and credit. Poverty in Rwanda thus has a female face. The country's Poverty Reduction Strategy Paper (PRSP) highlights that 62 per cent of female-headed households are under the poverty line compared to 54 per cent of male-headed households.

It is within this context that the Government of National Unity and Reconciliation has committed itself to tackle gender imbalances in all areas of life. In 1999, the President, Paul Kagame, expressed the commitment in these words at a seminar on gender and development:

> ... the abrupt shift to monetary economy, formal education and modern technology played a key role in restructuring gender relations to the disadvantage of women. These imbalances are not only an obstacle to the country's development but constitute a form of social injustice. It is therefore imperative to our lawmakers, policy makers and implementers to have an objective and correct analysis of the gender question in order to design appropriate corrective policies and programmes. The question of gender equality in our society needs a clear and critical evaluation in order to come up with concrete strategies to map the future development in which men and women are true partners and beneficiaries. My understanding of gender is that it is an issue of good governance, good economic management and respect of human rights

The government's political will was illustrated, among others, by the establishment in 1999 of the Ministry of Gender and Women in Development (MIGEPROFE, henceforward referred to as the gender ministry) a clear mission to promote gender equality and equity throughout the development policies of the country.

Objectives and Location of the Gender Budget Initiative

The Rwanda Gender Budget Initiative (GBI) takes forward the Government's political commitment to tackle gender imbalances. It starts from the standpoint that gender analysis is essential to the elaboration of budgets that enhance rather than hinder gender equality and human development in Rwanda. Its overarching objective is to translate into effective actions the government's commitment to promote gender equality and equality throughout the development process. The specific objectives of the GBI are:

◆ to inform the national debate about policy and the appropriate allocation of public resources;

◆ to ensure that the policies and programmes of ministries and provinces take into consideration the specific constraints, options, incentives and needs (COINs) of women and girls, men and boys; and

◆ to ensure that resources are allocated accordingly.

The GBI is consistent with the comprehensive system reforms that are being introduced to rebuild the country. The reforms and priorities are articulated around the following policy frameworks:

◆ Vision 2020, which indicates the national aspirations for the year 2020;

◆ the PRSP, which guides the national strategy and interventions for the reduction of poverty from 60% to 30%, by 2015;

◆ the Medium Term Expenditure Framework (MTEF), a coherent approach to budget management involving integrated, performance-related expenditure programmes formulated within a realistic three year resource framework;

◆ the National Gender Policy and Gender Plan of Action, which provide the strategic guideline for actions to promote gender equality and equity in all sectors;

◆ the decentralisation policy whose objective is to put the population at the heart of the decision-making and actions that shape their lives; and

◆ the elaboration of a new constitution and, more specifically, Rwanda's process of "engendering the new constitution" to promote a judiciary and legal system favourable to gender equality and equity.

The GBI is taking place within government. It is driven by the gender ministry in close collaboration with the Ministry of Finance and Economic Planning (MINECOFIN), henceforward referred to as the finance ministry). It is entirely funded by the United Kingdom's Department for International Development (DFID) through the Gender Mainstreaming and Development Programme housed at the gender ministry.

Approach and Strategies

The GBI focuses on expenditures and on the recurrent budget. At present 90 per cent of the development budget is donor-funded, compared to 40 per cent of the recurrent budget. Stakeholders thus felt that it was more appropriate to look only at the recurrent budget at this stage because government has far more control over this part than over the development budget. Further, the MTEF and other reforms are, for the moment, focusing on the recurrent budget. Work on the development budget and on revenue will be done later.

The activities of the Initiative were planned in line with the annual budget timetable. In particular, the first round of workshops was held before June 2002, which was when the finance ministry would set the framework for the 2003 budget.

The background document that sets out the plans for the GBI was informed by the analysis undertaken on different sectors by the gender ministry in 2000 and 2001 when drawing up the National Gender Policy and the National Gender Plan of Action. It was also informed by discussions between the gender ministry and actors such as the finance ministry, line ministries, provinces, women's organisations, other civil society organisations and development partners. The approach used was participatory and gradual, involving the finance ministry and line ministries right from the beginning of the GBI. The idea was to make line ministries commit themselves to and own the Initiative.

The GBI is based on strong collaboration between the ministries of gender and finance. This strategy was adopted on account of the important role assigned to the finance ministry in coordinating government's reforms and development priorities. The policy frameworks referred to above, such as Vision 2020, PRSP and MTEF, are all housed in and coordinated by that ministry and, consequently, unless its work is engendered, the engendering of government's budgets cannot be successful.

To build the collaboration, meetings and discussions were held between the ministries of gender and finance prior to the elaboration of the project and have continued throughout its implementation. These meetings have, at different times, involved a range of different parts of the finance ministry, namely the Directorate of Statistics, Directorate of Budgets, MTEF Unit, PRSP Unit and CEPEX, the national institution responsible for managing the development budget.

The GBI is being implemented through a pilot approach. It will be developed over a three-year period, from 2002 to 2004. By the last year, the budgets of all ministries and provinces should be engendered. In the first year, five ministries were selected to be pilots. In each subsequent year, the budgets of further ministries will be examined. The selection criteria for each year are informed by the PRSP priority actions and the relevance of gender issues in each sector.

The following pilot ministries were selected for participation in 2002 so as to be able to influence their 2003 budget:

◆ Ministry of Education

◆ Ministry of Agriculture

◆ Ministry of Health

◆ Ministry of Water and Energy

◆ Ministry of Local Government

Within each pilot ministry, the analysis focuses on those sub-programmes that have the biggest allocations.

The strategy of having pilot ministries is based on the realisation that engendering budgets requires a certain technical expertise. Given the limited capacity in this respect in ministries, it is essential to provide their officers with regular assistance throughout the process of elaboration of their budgets. Therefore, it is reasonable and efficient to select a limited number of ministries, at least for the first phase. Further, the experience during this pilot phase will inform future phases. We will learn from the strengths and weaknesses of the previous phases in order to improve future plans.

The Process

The Initiative consists of different steps which reinforce each other.

Preparing the ground

The first step was the organisation in January 2002 of a workshop on Engendering Budgets. The objective of the workshop was to prepare the ground for the Rwanda GBI. The event brought together senior officers working on budget elaboration and execution in line ministries and national institutions. Finance ministry staff from the Directorate of Budget, the Directorate of Statistics, CEPEX and the MTEF Unit attended the workshop and provided insights where necessary.

At this workshop, officers were informed about the relevance of integrating gender into their ministries' budgets and how to undertake such an exercise. They read case studies from Australia, Mexico, the Philippines, South Africa, Tanzania and Uganda, and discussed how these could be useful to the Rwandan case. Further, they made recommendations as to the pilot ministries to be selected for the first phase. Participants also emphasised the necessity of a close and continuous collaboration between the ministries of gender and finance.

The recommendations of participants were presented to the Minister of Gender and the Minister of Finance when the latter closed the workshop. The Minister of Finance seized this opportunity to reiterate his own commitment to the GBI. Meanwhile, he promised to ensure that his staff collaborated closely with staff at the gender ministry throughout the implementation of the Initiative.

The commitment of the Minister was important because it encouraged senior officers of the finance ministry to view working with staff at the gender ministry on engendering the government's budgets as part of their duties rather than as extra work. After the closing ceremony staff from both ministries met to evaluate the event and to plan the forthcoming activities of the Initiative.

Planning with the finance ministry

The second step was the organisation of a workshop for finance ministry officers. Participants came from the Directorate of Statistics, the Directorate of Budget, the MTEF Unit, the PRSP Unit and CEPEX. The objective of the workshop was threefold. Firstly, we wanted to provide the ministry's officers with refined tools and information on engendering budgets. Secondly, we wanted to discuss what gender issues mean for the ministry's work. Finally, we wanted to discuss the opportunities and challenges and plan the next steps.

During the workshop, the MTEF coordinator presented the objectives and progress of the framework. He highlighted the fact that it is a three-year budgetary framework through which ministries are provided with reliable ceilings within which to develop sector strategies and agreed outputs. It aims at:

- ◆ linking policies, plans and budgets;

- ◆ allowing informed choices amongst policies and objectives;

- ◆ increasing levels of efficiency and effectiveness; and

- ◆ increasing transparency of resource use against an agreed set of outputs.

Most of these points fit in well with gender budget work. Like the MTEF, the gender budget looks at prioritising, efficiency, transparency and linking policy with budgets. However, it adds consideration of equity of the budget allocations to these elements and thus brings an added value to the MTEF. As such, the MTEF and the gender budgets' objectives are consistent and reinforce each other.

The workshop enabled the finance ministry's officers to understand better the linkages between the gender budget approach and their work. However, there were two concerns. Officers feared that integrating gender into ministry budgets would entail a lot of new work which would not fit in with existing framework and reforms. They also feared that the budget document would become very long.

In response to these concerns, the strategy we used was to develop a concise format articulated around only the biggest sub-programmes of the respective ministries, using the MTEF and lessons learnt from the case studies of Australia, Malaysia and South Africa. Participants realised that the combination of focusing on only the largest sub-programmes and utilising such a format would not involve too much additional work and would only add six extra pages to their budget documents. This dampened their apprehension. It was agreed that the MTEF coordinator would present the following proposed format to the finance ministry's committee:

Table 11: Proposed format for the Rwanda gender budget

Programme (from the budget document)

Sub-programme and amount (from the budget document)

Gender issues: To describe the current situation. Use disaggregated statistics as much as possible.

Output 1 (from the budget document)

Activity 1 (from the budget document)
Activity 2 (from the budget document)
Activity 3 (from the budget document)

Output 1 indicators: (what will be measured in coming year)

Output 2 (from the budget document)
Activity 1 (from the budget document)
Activity 2 (from the budget document)
Activity 3 (from the budget document)
Output 2 indicators
Etc

The launch

The Prime Minister officially launched the GBI in March 2002. Twelve out of sixteen Ministers, together with Secretaries General, Members of Parliament, development partners, and members of civil society attended the gathering. The event was given widespread publicity by the national radio and television. In his remarks, the Prime Minister emphasised the importance that the government attached to the Initiative, which it saw as adding value to government's efforts toward poverty reduction. In so doing, the Prime Minister enshrined the government's willingness and commitment. Furthermore, he gave legitimacy and strong support to the GBI and reinforced the commitment of ministries' officers.

After the official launch, the guests left and Debbie Budlender, the South African consultant, and I co-facilitated a process which assisted officers from the pilot ministries in portfolio analysis and integration of gender concerns into their budgets. During the plenary sessions, participants were given the tools and logical process of engendering budgets, followed by practical exercises. The MTEF coordinator also presented the progress of the framework. In going through the exercises, we referred to the results of the participatory assessment of poverty and public expenditure carried out within the PRSP. We thus again pointed to the close links between the GBI and other reform processes.

The workshop aimed at producing a concrete product for each ministry, namely a gender budget statement related to the largest sub-programmes in the current budget. To achieve this, officers were asked to find out more about the sub-programmes which they had identified as the largest, and to search for disaggregated data on what the sub-programmes were doing. They were given an afternoon and morning in the middle of the workshop to go back to their offices to find the requested information. This was productive as officers were able to find and use more disaggregated information than we had known was available. During this time, we visited officers to monitor the progress of their work and give them assistance.

The officers then came together in another plenary session where they made presentations that were followed by inputs from their colleagues. The officers were advised to revise their presentations taking into account the suggestions and comments and submit them to the MTEF.

The strategy of asking officers to undertake an in-depth practical exercise was useful to evaluate:

◆ officers' understanding of the engendering budget framework;

◆ their capacity to undertake the exercise;

◆ their commitment; and

◆ the practicability of our proposed gender budget format.

The strategy helped us to refine the plan in collaboration with the MTEF coordinator and the Director of Budget, on the basis of the following observations:

◆ officers in all but one of the ministries took the assignment seriously;

◆ they were able to find relevant information and disaggregated data on their ministries' activities;

◆ they realised that using the gender budget format did not involve significant extra work, and it helped them to be more focused and to make their ministry's budget follow its mission and policy rather than vice versa;

◆ they nevertheless needed more assistance in gender analysis of the situation in which their ministries' programmes operate.

The workshop exercise was done on the basis of the 2002 budget. We were all aware that budgets tend to change very little from year to year and therefore hoped that this work would prepare the officers to apply their new insights in the formulation of their 2003 budgets later in the year. It was agreed that a gender budget document based on the format used at the workshop and focusing on the six largest sub-programmes of each pilot ministry would be presented as an annex to the 2003 budget document.

After the workshop, I provided support to the four ministries who reviewed their gender budget statements and submitted them to the MTEF. The fifth, despite reminders, did not appear to be either committed or interested.

Extending the Initiative to the provinces and non-governmental organisations

The next step was to hold a workshop for provinces on engendering budgets. This was important as the decentralisation policy adopted by Cabinet in 2000 is one of the Government's priorities. In particular, it is considered to be a strategic way to address "the inappropriate highly centralised dictatorial governance of the colonial as well as post independence administration of the country [which] excluded the Rwandese population from participating in the determination of their political, economic and administrative well-being" (Ministry of Local Government and Social Affairs, May 2000: 2). Moreover, the previous highly centralised approach to governance is seen as having contributed to the genocide.

Because of the political imperative, implementation of the decentralisation policy has happened faster in Rwanda than in most other African countries. Twelve provinces have been delineated, each of which encompasses between 15 and 20 districts. The latter are, in turn, divided into sectors and cells.

The provincial workshop on engendering budgets was held in May 2002. Eleven of the 12 provinces were represented by two senior officers each, namely the Executive Secretary and a Director (of planning or gender). The twelfth province could not attend as the President was visiting at that time.

The purpose of the provincial workshop was:

◆ to explain what the gender budget approach is about and how to apply it to their provinces' budgets;

◆ to share what had been done so far by pilot ministries and obtain their feedback; and

◆ to discuss the way forward, including how they could assist the districts.

Debbie Budlender and I again co-facilitated the event. Participants expressed great commitment to the Initiative. While they had limited formal background on gender, the fact that they work on the ground and thus are close to the communities helped them to understand the gender issues. They gave insights on how the budgets should match the populations' needs and provided a critical analysis of the work done by pilot ministries in March, making recommendations for improvement.

As at the previous workshops, the MTEF coordinator presented on the progress of the framework. The facilitators further emphasised the linkages between the MTEF and the gender budget. After this, the participants undertook an exercise on integrating gender issues into their provinces' budgets.

At the end of the workshop, participants made the following resolutions:

◆ to organise meetings in order to inform the provincial authorities about what they had learnt;

◆ to integrate gender issues into their 2003 budgets; and

◆ to assist districts in engendering their budgets.

The third decision was critical as the implementation of the decentralisation policy is moving quickly and it was not possible to cover all districts from the central level at this stage of the Initiative. Further, the participants suggested that the gender ministry participate in the planned provincial MTEF workshops to give an input on gender budgets. Unfortunately, due to limited capacity, it will not be able to follow up on this latter suggestion.

Immediately following the provinces' workshop, a one-day meeting was held for non-governmental organisations (NGOs) to:

◆ explain the relevance of integrating gender issues into the government's budget and how to undertake such an exercise;

◆ share with them the progress of the Rwanda GBI and work done by ministries and provinces; and

◆ discuss their role as civil society.

Attendance was good. There were 21 participants from both women's organisations and mixed NGOs dealing with legal issues, education, widows and women's entrepreneurship. The invitation was sent through PRO-FEMMES Twese Hamwe, which in turn sent individual invitations to its member organisations. PRO-FEMMES Twese Hamwe, which means 'all together' in Kinyarwanda, is the umbrella of national NGOs. It coordinates 41 organisations, of which the majority are women's NGOs.

After we explained to participants what the gender budget is about, they did an exercise on 'causes, consequences, solutions' in order to help them understand the gender analysis and mainstreaming framework. They discussed in groups the case studies of Australia, Mexico, the Philippines, South Africa, Tanzania and Uganda. They also criticised the work of the ministries and made recommendations for better integration of gender issues into the ministries' budgets for 2003. The case studies illustrated for them the role that NGOs played in initiatives in other countries and gave them an idea of what their role might be. Bolstered by these experiences, they made the following resolutions:

◆ to undertake research on the pilot ministries in order to document the impact of their budgets on women and men, girls and boys;

◆ to engage in advocacy and lobbying for the gender budget;

◆ to monitor and evaluate ministries and provinces' gender budgets; and

◆ to mobilise their own resources for such activities.

The establishment of alliances between the government and civil society is essential for the success and sustainability of the Rwanda GBI. Such alliances institutionalise the Initiative and prevent it from coming to a halt when there are changes in government, as was the case in Australia.

After the provinces' workshop and the NGO meeting, we evaluated the events and refined the plans for the future. Given the interest shown by the provinces' officers, we envisaged working more closely with three pilot provinces and assisting them in engendering their 2003 budgets. As the process goes along, further provinces and districts will be involved.

The selection of the three provinces will be informed by donor interventions in the implementation of the decentralisation policy, in that we will prioritise provinces where donors who are more likely to be interested in gender budget work are involved. This will create partnership with other donors in extending the Initiative to provinces and districts.

Fitting the Gender Budget into Other Related Processes

This year, as part of the development of the MTEF, the ministries are for the first time preparing strategic papers that give the background to, and justification for, their budgets. Gender is among several cross-cutting issues to be addressed in these papers. However, most officers do not know how to deal with it.

To address this issue, I prepared a handout explaining to ministries the relevance of integrating gender issues into their strategic papers and guiding them on how to do so. The process of elaboration of the strategic papers was discussed at a joint workshop organised by the MTEF, the PRSP and CEPEX. I attended and made a contribution at this event.

Strengths and Weaknesses of the GBI Process

The main strengths and weaknesses of the process undertaken so far to engender the Government of Rwanda's budgets can be summarised as follows.

Strengths

Politcal will There is strong political will at the highest level of the Government of Rwanda. This can be seen in concrete strategic actions such as those described above. The budget of a government expresses its priorities and choices. As pointed out by Debbie Budlender in the South African *Second Women's Budget* (1997 : 51), "any budget is intrinsically political. The budget determines from whom the state gets resources, and to whom and what it allocates them. Each decision is a political one, as is the decision on the overall size of the budget". This means that the political will and a decision to ensure that the government's budget meets the specific needs of women and men, girls and boys is the condition *sine qua non* of the success of the Rwanda GBI.

Gender awareness of staff of ministries Prior to the planning of the Rwanda GBI, the gender ministry undertook training on gender awareness for ministries and provinces. By now, officers in almost all ministries and provinces have been trained. This makes them sensitised to gender issues. We encountered little resistance during the workshops, although some clearly remains. This is evident, for example, in the passive resistance of the fifth ministry.

Strong involvement of the leadership of the gender ministry The Minister and the Secretary General of the gender ministry are very committed to the Initiative. They follow it seriously and give support where needed. For example, they contact ministries and provinces, opened the series of workshops and advocate at Cabinet level.

Existence of other reforms The fact that the Rwanda GBI is taking place alongside a set of reforms whose objectives are consistent with the gender budget creates a synergy that is conducive to the implementation of the Initiative.

Strong collaboration between the ministries of gender and finance The collaboration between the ministries of gender and finance has been built gradually through the process and is a key strength of the Initiative. The gender ministry is small and the fact that it collaborates with the finance ministry, which is considered very powerful, enhances its capacity to influence the government's budget. At the same time, the collaboration enables the gender ministry to sensitise the finance ministry on gender issues so that it can further engender its own work. This is important because, as noted by Gita Sen, "Finance ministry officials who are used to thinking in terms of macro financial variables, are likely to be somewhat at a loss when asked to engender their work" (1999: 31). The practical exercises undertaken with finance ministry officers convinced them of the relevance of integrating gender into their work. This extended beyond the immediate focus of the gender budget, which relates to the recurrent budget. For example, there was recognition on the part of the MTEF staff that their thinking around the public investment programme (PIP) needed to consider issues beyond growth. In particular, it needed to consider redistribution and unpaid labour.

Weaknesses

Limited capacity The limited expertise in general, and in gender analysis and gender mainstreaming in particular, is one of the critical weaknesses of the Initiative. This is one of the aftermaths of the 1994 genocide that destroyed the country's human resources. Although the officers have been sensitised to gender issues, it appeared during the different activities we undertook that they will need regular assistance on gender mainstreaming. The question of sustainability of the Initiative when I leave is also critical.

Staff turnover Staff turnover in ministries represents a risk as officers who have already been trained and involved in the process of engendering budgets might be lost. This will affect the sustainability of the Initiative.

Future Plans

The lessons learnt during the activities undertaken in the first phase of the initiative inform the future plans.

Collecting disaggregated data

Disaggregated data are critical to undertaking a gender analysis of the budgets of ministries and provinces. They provide a picture of the situation of women and men, girls and boys in each sector and in each province. They enable officers to highlight the gender issues related to their programmes.

Some data are available in surveys carried out between 1999 and 2001. These include the Household Living Conditions, the Core Welfare Indicators Questionnaire, the Tracking Expenditure on Education and Health study, the Demographic and Health survey, and the study on Cultural Beliefs, Attitudes and Practices in Relation to Gender in Rwanda.

The gender ministry has worked with the Directorate of Statistics and the Poverty Observatory Unit to ensure that most of the data are disaggregated. However, we realised during the workshops that officers did not necessarily know about the data. Further, they were not aware of all the administrative data available in their own offices. It was only once they went back to the ministries specifically to look for it that they discovered quite a lot of data.

To address this, actions will be taken to disseminate disaggregated statistics widely. I am currently working with the Directorate of Statistics and the Poverty Observatory Unit on a compilation of disaggregated data on the situation of women and men, girls and boys in each sector. We hope to finish and distribute this booklet by mid-year. The booklet will be an important tool for the officers in ministries and provinces.

Preparing budgets for 2003

It is envisaged that I will assist the ministries throughout the elaboration of their budgets for 2003. After the pilot ministries and provinces have completed their 2003 budgets, a book will be published to document and disseminate what has been done so far. The report will be officially launched by the ministries of gender and finance.

Before or after the official launch, the 2002 (first) phase of the Initiative will be evaluated by the officers from the pilot ministries and provinces who were responsible for preparing their gender budget statements. The evaluation will explore how the process of the Initiative can be improved for the next phases and how the pilot ministries' approach should move forward.

A donors' meeting will be organised to present the progress of the Initiative and get their feedback. The meeting will be an opportunity to discuss the possibility of starting to integrate gender into the development budget. The event will be held around the time of the annual meeting between the Government and development partners in November 2002.

Bibliography

Budlender D. (1997) *The Second Women's Budget*. Institute for Democracy in South Africa, Cape Town.

Sen G. (1999) *A Quick Guide to Gender Mainstreaming in Finance*. Commonwealth Secretariat, London.

Ministry of Local Government and Social Affairs (2000) *Implementation Strategy for National Decentralisation Policy*. Kigali.

Scotland: Using political change to advance gender concerns

Ailsa McKay, Rona Fitzgerald, Angela O'Hagan and Morag Gillespie[4]

Table 12: Selected Indicators for Scotland

Indicator	Year	Number
Population	2000	5,115,000
% of population which is female	2000	51.4
% of population which is urban	1999	90.8
Gross domestic product per (GDP) capita (US$)		n/a
Human development index (HDI)		n/a
Gender development index (GDI)		n/a
% of total budget funded by donors	2002	0%
% of national parliamentarians who are women	2000	37

Introduction

The Scottish experience of promoting gender-sensitive budgeting occurs against a background of significant institutional and policy changes. The key change has been the establishment of the devolved Scottish Parliament in May 1999. The Scottish Parliament is made up of 129 elected members (MSPs) and operates as a self-contained and full parliament in its own right. Thus it both passes legislation and scrutinises the work of the Scottish Executive, which was established in 1999 following the first parliamentary elections. It is responsible for most of the issues of day-to-day concern to the people of Scotland, including health, education, justice, rural affairs and transport, and manages an annual budget of around £20 billion. It is led by a First Minister who in turn appoints the other ministers.

[4] All authors are members of the Engender Women's Budget Group (EWBG). Further information about Engender and its activities can be found on their website – http://www.engender.org.uk/index.html

This chapter outlines how the collective efforts of a group of active campaigners led to the promotion of the issue of gender-sensitive budgeting in Scottish political debate. In addition, it outlines the steps that have been taken to embark on a gender budget initiative within the newly devolved administration. The Scottish story does not provide concrete examples of gender-sensitive budgeting in practice in terms of shifts in policy priorities. It does, however, provide insights into how a changing political environment has been used to advance concerns relating to gender inequalities in general and how new partnerships have been forged in the process, both within government and externally. Further, there is now a publicly stated commitment to "assess the equality impact of spending plans and decisions as part of the mainstreaming agenda" (Scottish Executive, 2000:17).

The chapter tells the story of the Engender Women's Budget Group (EWBG). The first section outlines the nature of political change in Scotland and describes how EWBG came about. The second section details key developments that have taken place since devolution, in relation to adopting a gender-sensitive approach to budgeting. The final section identifies planned future activities and assesses both the strengths and weaknesses of the Scottish experience to date.

Embracing Change: Devolution in Scotland and the Evolution of the EWBG

Scotland has a total population of just over 5 million. In terms of gender inequalities, women are poorer than men, live longer than men, disproportionately share the burden of caring work, both paid and unpaid, and are under-represented in positions of power. It follows that women in Scotland are in a disadvantaged socio-economic position when compared with their male counterparts.

Although the progress made in Scotland in respect of gender-sensitive budgeting can be clearly linked with the favourable political framework that predated devolution, the influence of external forces at both UK and international level should not be discounted. The beginning of the new millennium marked a period of significant political and economic change in Scotland, which served to present women activists in the country with an opportunity to work together and make a difference.

The new Scottish Parliament and Executive

The May 1997 UK general election represented a significant milestone for Scotland in that devolution – the transfer of power to a Scottish parliament and executive for a number of policy areas – now seemed likely to become a political reality. Following their election victory the New Labour government arranged for a referendum to be held on 11 September 1997 on its proposals for a Scottish parliament. and the Scottish electorate produced a clear majority in favour. The first Parliament took up its full legislative powers in July 1999. Today, it has responsibility for some functions, while non-devolved functions remain the responsibility of the UK Parliament at Westminster. Equal opportunities in employment is among the non-devolved functions.

The Scottish budget

The Scottish budget process involves three main stages: the setting of priorities and expenditure strategy; the presentation of detailed expenditure proposals in the publication of the draft budget; and the enactment of the budget bill.

The Scottish Parliament has the power to vary the standard rate of income tax, but the current administration has chosen not to use this power. The current emphasis is therefore on the public spending allocation process. The budget process of the newly devolved administration was designed in such a way as to promote open annual budgeting and accommodate the enhanced scrutiny role of the Parliament. As a result, public consultation has become a key feature of the way the Executive determines its spending priorities.

Women embrace change: The Equality Agenda and structures of the new institutions

The planned establishment of the Scottish Parliament in May 1999 brought with it increased opportunities to influence the policy-making process, because of the commitment to consultation and transparency. Women's groups across Scotland embraced this opportunity. The women's movement became more positive about the opportunities for women and gender equality that devolved government offered, and became closely involved in the pro-devolution campaigns in the period May 1997 to 1999. Many of the women involved were well placed to access senior politicians and decision makers because of their positions in public bodies, universities, trade unions and other aspects of public life. Formal and informal networks were facilitated by the fact that Scotland is a relatively small country with a dense urban population.

The subsequent establishment of the Parliament and Executive represented a window of opportunity for the women's lobby. The absence of a stated political commitment to gender in election manifestos suggests that the promotion of gender balance and gender mainstreaming in Scotland can be directly attributed to the lobbying and participation of women's groups throughout the process towards devolution.

As noted above, equal opportunities in employment is a non-devolved function. However, the promotion of equal opportunities for all is one of the key stated principles guiding the work of the new Executive and Parliament. The work of the Consultative Steering Group (CSG) was key in reaching this situation. The CSG was appointed by the Secretary of State for Scotland in November 1997 to bring together a range of views and to develop proposals for the practical operation of the new Parliament. Its membership was representative of the major political parties in Scotland and of other civic groups and interests. The report of the CSG recommended a model of governance where the concepts of sharing power, accountability, access, participation and equal opportunities would be paramount. Annex H of the Report endorsed the evidence submitted by the Equal Opportunities Commission (EOC), Scotland and clearly states that "the aim must be to embed into the process of policy formulation and the way in which the Parliament works, the principles and commitment to promote equal opportunities for all and to eliminate the effects of past discrimination" (Consultative Steering Group, 1998:146).

In addition to the favourable framework provided by endorsing a mainstreaming approach to policy, the actual operation of the new Parliament is key in understanding the progress made to date in promoting gender-sensitive budgeting in Scotland. Much of the Parliament's work is conducted through a committee system. A number of key committees are required by the standing orders, including the Finance Committee and the Equal Opportunities Committee. Further committees can be established to deal with a particular subject or area of public policy. Adopting a committee structure was intended to enhance accountability, access and participation. The committees play a central role in ensuring that there is wide consultation on proposed legislation, in encouraging public involvement in the Parliament's activities, and in holding the Scottish Executive to account. The emphasis on consultation and scrutiny has provided interested parties with an important access point for the purpose of influencing policy debates.

The Equal Opportunities Committee of the Parliament and the Equality Unit of the Executive have provided foci to promote a mainstreaming approach to policy. The committee acts as a catalyst to ensure that equality plans and targets are outlined for all the committees, and that effective monitoring systems are put in place. The Equality Unit outlined its plan for achieving equality in its *Equality Strategy: Working together for Equality*, published in November 2000 following a period of widespread consultation. The strategy provides a new context for the search for equality in Scotland. A generic approach has been adopted in that equal opportunities is understood in its broadest sense with reference to race, disability and gender. In addition, issues around age discrimination, sexual orientation, religion and travelling people are specifically included in the definition of equal opportunities in the Scotland Act of 1998. The *Equality Strategy* commits the Scottish Executive to mainstreaming equality in policy making by setting out a number of key actions and target completion dates for initiatives. One such initiative is to develop mechanisms for assessing the equality impact of budgets and spending plans. The inclusion of this specific action plan can be directly linked to the campaigning efforts of the EWBG.

The evolution of a Scottish Women's Budget Group

As previously noted, the establishment of the devolved Parliament brought with it increased opportunities to engage with the political agenda. In recognition of this, the women's organisation Engender organised a seminar to consult with as many interested groups and individuals as possible on the setting up of a women's budget group.

Engender is an information, research and networking organisation for women in Scotland. It works with other groups locally and internationally to improve women's lives and increase their power and influence. The organisation campaigns to ensure that women and their concerns have greater visibility and equal representation at all levels of Scottish society. The organisation is 10 years old and has over 300 women members from across Scotland and from a diverse range of backgrounds.

137

The seminar took place in Edinburgh in November 1999. There was representation from a range of women's organisations, from the Equality Unit and from the office of the Parliament's Finance Committee convenor. The seminar was addressed by a member of the England-based UK Women's Budget Group (WBG). There was a useful exchange of information regarding how best to proceed in Scotland with promoting the issue of gender-sensitive budgeting within the new political framework.

The main issue raised at the seminar was that, although there was a growing body of literature relating to gender budget initiatives, the situation in Scotland was unique. Firstly, the political institutions were at a very early stage of development and there was uncertainty as to how procedures and operating structures would evolve over time. Secondly, as the new administration had opted not to use its tax varying powers, issues of revenue raising were irrelevant for the time being. Thus the annual budget statement would essentially be an expenditure statement. The focus on expenditure, although not unusual in international terms, means that the Scottish budget process and statement are different from those at a UK national level. The seminar participants recognised the importance of the exchange of information, practice and tools. However, it was apparent that there was great deal to be done in building capacity regarding the nature of our own new political environment.

Soon after this initial seminar, the Finance Department of the Executive produced a consultation document containing proposals for the first round of spending allocation for 2000/1 and 2001/2. The consultation exercise presented the nascent EWBG with an immediate focus. Although the group was not formally constituted, a number of interested individuals collectively prepared a response commenting on the gender impact of specific proposals and calling for the establishment of a framework incorporating gender impact analysis within the budget process. The purpose of the response was not to conduct a full gender audit of the spending proposals, given that the group did not have the resources to engage in such an exercise. Instead, we set out the rationale for gender-responsive budgeting practices and pointed out how such a strategy would conform with the overall objective of mainstreaming equality.

Since EWBG did not yet formally exist, we decided to submit the response from Engender, which was already well established as a credible women's organisation. Engender explicitly offered its own services, as follows:

> We propose that the Scottish Executive set in place a mechanism which would allow for a more detailed assessment of particular spending plans with reference to the impact such have on women. On our part we are prepared to convene a group of Scottish experts who can comment on the gendered nature of the Scottish spending proposals. We would welcome the opportunity to get involved in regular dialogue with the Scottish Executive on this issue, with a view to establishing a formal process of ensuring that future spending proposals take account of gender differences. (Engender, 1999)

The submission was received with interest and referred to by the Minister for Finance in his opening statement presenting the first budget bill to parliament:

> …Our consultation has also given us new ideas and ways in which to improve the budget processes. For example, the group Engender – which, as its name implies, is concerned with gender issues – suggested that we needed to conduct a gender audit across our spending programmes, to assess their overall impact on women. I have told it that I intend to develop that idea for the future (Minister for Finance, 26 January 2000).

Representatives of Engender were subsequently invited to give evidence before different parliamentary committees and to meet with the Minister for Finance to discuss proposals for ensuring that gender impact analysis becomes an integral feature of the spending allocation process. The invitation to present evidence to the Local Government Committee was largely due to the influence of the then convenor of the Finance Committee. Two factors were at work here. Firstly, his parliamentary researcher had attended the Edinburgh seminar and is a key player in both accessing and informing senior politicians. Secondly, the then convenor was identified as one of our 'champions' in that he was very supportive of the case for gender-sensitive budgeting. Subsequently, during his time as convenor he encouraged the Finance Committee to account for gender in its scrutiny role. This approach filtered out to the other committees. An additional reason for our invitation to present to committees was the activity of a supportive female MSP who at the time was a member of both the Local Government and Equal Opportunities Committees.

During discussions in the committee meetings, continual reference was made to the international experience and how Scotland could benefit from examining how other countries had approached this administratively difficult area. Representatives of Engender responded by noting that the Scottish situation was unique and caution should be exercised in trying to mimic another country's approach. Rather, the focus should be on developing an understanding of the Scottish policy process and tailoring any existing approaches.

In making this point, members of Engender drew on relevant Scottish-based research. In particular they drew on a report on equality proofing legislation which had been commissioned by the Scottish Executive and carried out by Governance of Scotland Forum (Mackay & Bilton, 2001). Gender proofing can be defined as a process of checking a policy proposal to ensure that potential gender discriminatory effects have been avoided and that gender equality is promoted. Engender argued that, although there is now a growing body of literature supporting the case for gender-sensitive budgeting and identifying a range of generic tools, relevant examples of gender proofing in action are limited.

Furthermore, with reference to existing international literature Engender pointed out that, whilst the emerging tendency in Scotland appeared to be a focus on a broad-based equality approach, more work has been done on gender impact assessment models than on generic equality issues. Drawing from international experience, it would therefore seem that adopting a gender-sensitive approach to the budget process would be a useful starting point. In making this argument, the point was stressed that the focus on generic equality issues is worthwhile and should be retained for the long run.

The Scottish Executive have taken as their focus equal opportunities in the broadest sense – including race, disability and gender. The concern among women's groups like Engender is that this broad focus downplays the importance of gender. The groups maintain that gender as a lens can help identify other inequalities relating to race, religion, disability and age. Addressing gender in the first instance would provide insights into the social construction of inequality and how discriminatory practices can sustain and even promote inequity. This would aid in the process of developing an understanding of the nature of a whole range of inequalities. Efforts on behalf of Engender to promote gender as a starting point have been sustained but tension around this issue is yet to be resolved.

A meeting with the Minister for Finance was arranged. The meeting was facilitated by the then Director of the EOC, reflecting the greater access to senior politicians in the new Scotland. This meeting proved invaluable in securing the support and commitment of the Minister to the concept of gender budgets. Further, one of the key outcomes of this meeting was a stated commitment to establish a Scottish Executive advisory group with a focus on promoting this agenda.

In addition to the support evidenced from within government, these early meetings with parliamentarians indicated positive cross-party political interest in ensuring that future policy debates incorporate a gender impact analysis, particularly with reference to the budget statement. There is a strong commitment in the founding principles of the Scottish Parliament to cross-party consensus rather than conflict politics. Further, the cross-party nature of the parliamentary committees provides a framework for the building of political alliances. Such a framework is enhanced by the structures of the new Parliament that allow for topic-specific cross-party groups. One such group, the Scottish Parliament's Cross Party Group on Women was established by the EOC Scotland to act as a networking group for women MSPs. The group has been particularly supportive of the work of Engender. Many of the women MSPs were personally known to women activists, and in particular members of EWBG, in that they themselves had a history in the women's movement in Scotland. The Cross-Party Group gave these newly elected politicians a chance to remain in contact with external groups and provided a valuable access point for groups like Engender.

Given this apparent political interest and stated political will, members of Engender, together with a number of additional interested women, began establishing networks of contacts, gathering relevant literature and developing expertise on gender impact analysis and the budget process. The range and concentration of this activity gave rise to the need to formalise the Scottish group and to develop a working strategy. Subsequently the Engender Women's Budget Group (EWBG) was formally constituted in May 2000. We decided to link the group explicitly with Engender in order create continuity with our early written evidence, and also to utilise the existing credibility of Engender.

EWBG is an autonomous sub-group of Engender with members from statutory organisations, trade unions, the voluntary sector and higher education. EWBG's work was not originally funded and members contribute on a voluntary basis. Funding has, however, recently been secured from Oxfam to employ a part-time parliamentary liaison worker. This person was appointed in March 2002 for a period of 12 months.

EWBG held a half-day seminar in October 2000 for the purpose of developing a strategic approach in future activities. The meeting came up with the following strategy:

◆ To build on existing expertise within the group of the budgetary and mainstreaming process.

◆ To develop new political relationships within Scotland and to keep a watching brief on parliamentary bills.

◆ To support the establishment of the Scottish Executive Equality Proofing Budgets Advisory Group (EPBAG) and ensure EWBG's active participation in it.

◆ To develop mechanisms for consulting with different types of women's groups to ensure statements about policy impacts were rooted in the experience of women in the community.

◆ To focus on the areas of housing, childcare, enterprise and lifelong learning with a view to highlighting the relationship between policy, the budget statement and actual impact.

◆ To liaise with the England-based UK Women's Budget Group (WBG) on the gender impact of tax and benefit policies.

EWBG Engages with the New Institutions

Building a knowledge base: EWBG learns from others

In the first twelve months following the establishment of EWBG, its activities have been mainly reactive. Because most members contribute to the group in a voluntary capacity when their other commitments allow, activities have been limited to keeping up with current budget debates, responding to relevant consultation documents and invitations to meetings with officials and ministers, and giving evidence at committees. Further, the period has been used to build capacity within EWBG by holding internal workshops on gender impact analysis and how this methodology can be applied to national budgeting practices. With initial support from the EOC, Scotland, EWBG has regularly been able to send a representative to meetings of the WBG. As an infant organisation, expertise within EWBG has still to grow whereas the England-based group is well established. Thus the main purpose of attending the London meetings was to build capacity within EWBG and to establish lines of communication between the two groups.

In practice, our presence at the London meetings has proved invaluable in terms of a two-way exchange of experience. One example of this was when a member of EWBG was invited to attend a meeting with officials at the UK's Treasury Department, along with members of the WBG. The meeting drew on the Scottish experience as an example of how effective the consultation process could be in promoting the issue of gender-sensitive budgeting and drawing attention to the gender-blind nature of many budget proposals.

Despite the reactive nature of most activities, a number of significant developments have occurred which can be attributed to the proactive efforts of members of EWBG, either representing the group or acting in their work-related capacities. These include:

◆ Establishing a network of contacts on an international level. Thus two academic members of the group are currently working with the Basque government in preparing a manual and series of training days on gender-sensitive budgets; two representatives of the group attended the OECD/UNIFEM conference in Brussels in October 2001 on gender-responsive budgeting; one member of EWBG is also a member of the International Association for Feminist Economics (IAFFE) and, in attending various IAFFE conferences, has established contact with a number of international experts in the field of gender budgeting; and representatives of EWBG initiated and assisted in the organisation of a two-day seminar featuring international speakers hosted by the Executive's Equality Unit on gender-responsive budgeting practices.

◆ Arranging the programme for a seminar addressed by representatives of the Canadian government and the convenor of the Scottish Parliament's Finance Committee, examining the long Canadian experience of gender impact analysis across the public policy process.

◆ An EWBG member securing funding from Glasgow Caledonian University to investigate methods of gender proofing budgets with a view to establishing a framework applicable in the Scottish context.

◆ Submitting a successful proposal to the Equality Unit to investigate the budgetary process in operation within the new Scottish administration.

The most significant development has been the securing of funding for a part-time worker. The availability of a paid worker will ease some of the burden on existing members and allow a more proactive approach in campaigning efforts. In particular, it will enable a more coordinated approach to responding to the Parliament, based on consensus about the issues involved. It will also provide a degree of continuity that will enable us to return to previous debates and statements of intent.

All of the above activities constitute progress towards building capacity within EWBG. In the period from May 2000 a great deal of learning and knowledge sharing has occurred via comparative research and talking to others. The way the group has operated to date is representative of a long tradition in the women's movement in Scotland of consulting widely, using case studies and generally learning and sharing.

Gaining access to government

One of the main successes of EWBG has been the group's access to senior politicians and government officials and the establishment of working relationships with key players in the Scottish policy-making community. Much of what we have achieved in this area is directly attributable to informal contacts and the increased accessibility brought about by the devolution settlement. The devolved administration has embraced a more open and inclusive approach to governance, and politicians are now closer both geographically and to the issues. EWBG has capitalised on this new political environment.

In some cases the political support that we have achieved has been the result of circumstances beyond our control. We have benefited, in particular, from personal contacts at senior level in the newly created Equality Unit. The head of the unit has facilitated access to senior officials in the Finance Department of the Executive and a working relationship with some of the officials has evolved. We thus continue to operate on two levels with reference to accessing government. Firstly, we engage with the Parliament through MSPs, ministers and the parliamentary committees. Secondly, we have forged working relationships with senior civil servants within the Equality Unit and in the Finance Department.

In forging these links, EWBG has identified 'champions'. These are politicians who expressed support at an early stage for our proposals. They have included the convenor of the Finance Committee and the Minister for Finance. The support of these two men has undeniably contributed to the speed with which progress has been made. Although support has been voiced by a number of women MSPs, the fact that EWBG was able to influence such senior men is key.

Despite the relatively young age of the devolved government, there has been a great deal of change at a political level. The unfortunate death of the First Minister in October 2000, and the resignation of his successor the following year, resulted in ministerial reshuffles and shifts in committee membership. EWBG has had to keep up with such changes and re-establish relationships with new players. The current situation has worked in our favour in that key positions are now filled by identified 'champions'. For example, the incumbent First Minister in his previous post as Minister for Finance was one of our early supporters. Further, the previous convenor of the Finance Committee has been promoted to a ministerial position and has transferred his support for gender-sensitive budgeting to issues relating to his ministerial portfolio. The new convenor of the Finance Committee is known to members of EWBG and has expressed his eagerness to continue with progress made by his predecessor.

Although access is crucial, EWBG is aware of the pitfalls of informal arrangements and has experienced both the negative and positive effects of political change. A more formal approach to our working relationships with the new institutions has been established through the Equality Proofing Budgets Advisory Group.

The Equality Proofing Budgets Advisory Group (EPBAG)

> Best value is for all.... Equality proofing will be embedded in the detailed processes of departmental spending and the secondment of research help. The advisory group that we will announce soon will take that forward (Scottish Executive Minister for Finance, 20 September 2000)

The creation of an advisory group to further an equality proofing budgets agenda was raised by the Minister for Finance at one of the early meetings with EWBG. Subsequently the Equality Proofing Budgets Advisory Group (EPBAG) was set up by the Executive in November 2000 to support the development of a programme of work promoting

145

equality proofing of the Scottish budget. The group comprises representatives from the EOC, the Commission for Racial Equality, the Disability Rights Commission, the Equality Network, the Finance Department, the Equality Unit and EWBG.

EWBG's experience of involvement in this group has to date been generally positive. However, tensions have arisen around the equality vs. gender debate referred to above and much of the discussion at meetings has focused on this. Although sometimes frustrating, these discussions have proved useful in building capacity within the Executive on gender concerns in general and on methods of gender impact assessment.

Two main developments are directly attributable to the activities of EPBAG. Firstly, the Equality Unit hosted a two-day seminar aimed at raising awareness and exchanging information on engendering budgets. Secondly, EPBAG commissioned research to investigate the nature of the budgetary process in Scotland with a view to identifying next steps in developing a gender-sensitive approach in the allocation of public resources. This research was considered necessary because the budget process in Scotland is unique, given the new political environment. The published proceedings from the seminar and the publication of the research report will prove valuable resources for a range of individuals and organisations across Scotland.

Among the issues identified in the report (Fitzgerald & McKay, 2002) are the following:

◆ The newly devolved administration in Scotland provides an opportunity for innovative approaches to the equitable allocation of public resources.

◆ Strategies for enhancing the role of the budget in mainstreaming equalities include increased recognition of the Spending Review in the budget process; a commitment to outcome-based budgeting; the addition of advisory and scrutiny roles for the Finance Department and Committee; and the appointment of a specialist advisor to comment on equality impacts of policy.

◆ International examples of good practice in the integration of gender mainstreaming and the public policy process could inform the coordination of longer term inter-departmental initiatives in Scotland.

The establishment of EPBAG is representative of the new politics in

Scotland in that ad-hoc advisory groups which draw on specific expertise are part of the Executive's commitment to consultation and participation. EWBG welcomes the opportunity to engage with the executive via EPBAG. Furthermore our involvement in this group has strengthened our working relationship with the Equality Unit.

Scrutinising the annual expenditure report (AER)

> I want to continue to improve it [the AER] both in terms of its con-tent and presentation and in shifting the emphasis more towards what we achieve with expenditure rather than the amount we spend … we can learn from the experience of other countries in the dealing with both equality in budgeting and budgeting for out-comes….We should see incremental improvement in next year's aer in terms of its dealing with equality matters… I am very keen that this becomes embedded in our policy process and that the policy flows through into Finance. (Minister for Finance and Local Government, letter to Finance Committee, August 2001).

The start of the 2003/4 budget round commenced with the publication of the annual expenditure report (AER) at the end of March 2002. EWBG set about preparing its response. We were generally disappointed with the lack of gender-related information contained within the AER documents, particularly given that we were aware of guidance, issued by the Finance Department, asking departments to demonstrate the progress made in taking forward the mainstreaming equality agenda.

However, what is pleasing about this round as opposed to our past experience is how our response has made an impact on the scrutiny role of the committees. We have been called to give evidence at the Equal Opportunities Committee, who have quoted from our oral evidence and included the full text of our submission as an appendix to their report to the Finance Committee. In addition we have been consulted by the newly appointed advisor to the Finance Committee for the purpose of clarifying issues we raised in our response. We subsequently prepared a series of written answers to his questions and remain in regular dialogue with him and thus with the Finance Committee.

EWBG's collective efforts in responding to the 2003/4 AER have been enhanced by the activities of the newly-appointed development worker. A series of meetings have been arranged with MSPs who are committee members to investigate how best to proceed within the committee structures. An issue identified at the first meeting was the desire for guidance about questions to assist with the scrutiny process. Subsequent questions raised by MSPs were based on some loosely drafted questions prepared at their request by EWBG members.

An analysis of the scrutiny debate for the 2003/4 spending round indicates a considerable amount of debate on gender impact assessment, much of it arising as a direct result of EWBG's activities. The Finance Committee has subsequently stated they would like to see "meaningful progress with the equality strategy as it is one of the fundamental principles underpinning the Parliament" (Finance Committee, 2002).

It is unlikely that there will be any significant changes to the budget for 2003/4 as a result of that debate, but it does lay the ground for higher expectations in the future. A crucial feature of EWBG's activities will thus involve exploring ways in which committees can be better informed about the gender impact of particular spending allocations in advance of the next budget round.

The Future for EWBG: A Long-term Strategy

Understanding the budgetary process

Given the relative 'newness' of the Scottish administration, an essential first step in the process of working towards gender-responsive budgeting is to make the nature of the budget process explicit. Although the highly political nature of the budget process is understood, developing an understanding of key stages and players in the process is vital to the agenda of promoting transparency in the resource allocation process.

Research carried out for EPBAG has increased knowledge of the budget process in Scotland and how it relates to the UK budget statement among EWBG members and decision-makers within the Executive and Parliament. This promotes the dual objectives of ensuring transparency and accountability in the budget process. The intention is to ensure that this research is disseminated to as wide an audience as possible for the purpose of building capacity, both internally and on an external level.

Widening participation and building capacity

An early priority in future work plans is the development of mechanisms for consulting with different types of women's groups in order to ensure that statements about policy impacts become rooted in the experience of women in the community. Within EWBG there is already a great deal of knowledge, skill and expertise. It would be in keeping with the ethos of the group to share that knowledge in order to build a collective understanding of the issues rather than to look to outside 'experts' for their analysis. The group has identified the need to produce leaflets and other information as part of a wider strategy on awareness raising involving outreach work, briefing materials and media work.

Scrutinising the AER

The scrutinising role of the committees of the new parliament has been an important and developing area of engagement for EWBG. Although the capacity of committees to fulfil the role of scrutinising legislation and budgets with regard to gender impact was limited in the early stages, increased knowledge and experience have combined with greater engagement with EWBG to ensure that more robust scrutiny develops. EWBG has developed strong informal links with MSPs and has submitted oral and written evidence to several committees. In the current budget round, some committees have asked questions that have ensured that issues around equality mainstreaming in general, and gender-sensitive budgeting in particular, remain important concerns for the Parliament. The questions have elicited information from departments about their progress in developing gender-sensitive or gender-specific targets in their budget plans. These lay the ground for mapping future progress and will assist committees in seeking to hold the Executive to account for progress made.

Sustainable relationships

Much of EWBG's contact with politicians and civil servants has been informal. Although this has been helpful in breaking down barriers, there is a need to build more formal links through EPBAG and formal meetings with ministers and advisers over the next year. EWBG's limited resources have meant that engagement with groups of women in communities across Scotland has been restricted. We recognise that building support amongst women in Scotland is an important part of future policy development.

Conclusion

Identifying an appropriate gender budget initiative in Scotland at this point in time is not only desirable but also entirely in keeping with the current overarching principles of the newly devolved administration. The political context in Scotland provides the opportunity for embracing new and innovative approaches to governance. The change in the political climate is accompanied by a stated commitment to advance an agenda of anti-discriminatory principles in all walks of private and public life. The opportunity exists for effective collaboration between researchers, NGOs, parliamentarians and government officials to ensure a more fair and equitable allocation of public resources.

The experience in Scotland during the first few years of the newly devolved administration has demonstrated a strong desire to engage in participative and consultative governance. EWBG has capitalised on this new political environment and has seized the opportunity to engage with both the Scottish Executive and the Parliament in an attempt to ensure that gender concerns are embedded within the Scottish policy process. Results to date have been positive and it seems that gender concerns are now considered a priority with reference to budget choices. Although the immediate focus has been on the budget, significant developments are ongoing with regard to the general agenda of mainstreaming. EWBG feels that the Scottish story is worth telling in that it provides evidence of women's groups creating change in the way public policy-making is approached.

References

Consultative Steering Group on the Scottish Parliament (1998). *Shaping Scotland's Parliament*. Edinburgh, The Scottish Office.

Engender (1999) "Response to the Consultation Document Covering the Financial Plans for 2000–01 to 2001–02." *Engender*, 15 December.

Finance Committee (2002). "Report Stage 1 of the 2003/04 Budget Process." 18 June.

Fitzgerald, Rona (1999). *Toolkit for Mainstreaming Equal Opportunities in the European Structural Funds: A Practical Guide to Plan Preparation and Implementation*. Scottish Executive, Equal Opportunities Commission (Scotland) and HERA.

Fitzgerald R. and A. McKay (2002). *Understanding the Scottish Budgetary Process*. Report Submitted to Scottish Executive, Equality Unit, February 2002.

Mackay F. and K. Bilton (2001). *Equality Proofing Procedures in Drafting Legislation: International Comparisons*. Governance of Scotland Forum.

Scottish Executive (2000). *Equality Strategy: Working Together for Equality*. November.

South Africa: Expanding into diverse initiatives

Debbie Budlender, Janine Hicks and Lisa Vetten

Table 13: Selected Indicators for South Africa

Indicator	Year	Number
Population	1996	40.6 million
% of population which is female	1996	52%
% of population which is urban	1996	54%
Gross domestic product (GDP) per capita (US$)	1999	8,908
Human development index (HDI)	1999	0.702
Gender development index (GDI)	1999	0.695
% of total budget funded by donors	1998	2%
% of national parliamentarians who are women	2002	30%

Introduction

South Africa was one of the first countries to have a gender budget initiative. While Australia's initiative was introduced in the mid-1980s, it was only in the middle of the next decade – in 1995 – that initiatives emerged in other countries, namely in the Philippines and South Africa. In Australia and the Philippines, the initiative was based inside government. In South Africa, the initiative began outside government, as a collaborative venture of women parliamentarians and non-governmental organisations (NGOs). The collaboration became known as the Women's Budget Initiative (WBI).

The development of the core South African initiative has been described elsewhere. (See, for example, Budlender, 2000.) The WBI has also produced a range of publications which record the findings of its research. This chapter will not repeat what has been covered before except insofar as it provides background for what we describe here. Instead, it focuses on an aspect in which the South African situation differs from that in many other countries, namely the extent to which the idea of the gender budget approach has taken root beyond the core initiative. To name just one example, gender budget analysis is included in curricula at several South African universities, with the WBI's books as prescribed reading.

The developments described in this chapter were not foreseen when the partners embarked on the gender budget journey in 1995. Indeed, at the outset the project was seen very much as an experimental project – one that might be abandoned if it proved impossible or unfruitful. The approach used in the first pilot year did, however, plant the seeds for later developments. In particular, the core partners in the WBI involved a number of different stakeholders in the initiative from the start. The core partners did not do the research themselves but instead approached people in NGOs and academia with knowledge of the different sectors to do it. Further, they set up an advisory team of people with sectoral and other relevant knowledge. When the first year's research was complete and compiled into a report, the publication was launched through a well-attended event which was opened by the Deputy Minister of Finance and attended by a wide range of stakeholders.

The original WBI was conceived as a research and advocacy initiative. Basically, the NGO partners would be primarily responsible for research which revealed gender aspects of policy and related budgets, and parliamentarians would use the findings to advocate for a better deal. As the initiative developed, however, we perceived both the shortcomings in this original conception and a range of possibilities which had not been seen at the beginning. In this chapter we look at four different ways in which gender budget work has expanded beyond the original players and beyond the original products.

Section 1 looks at the development of workshop materials. We consider this important as, while workshops are a common feature of virtually all gender budget initiatives, there has been very little focused activity on generating materials. Section 2 looks at gender budget work focused on violence against women. We include this to illustrate how this work, rather than starting with a focus defined by how government is organised – for example a ministry – can start with a 'problem' or gender issue. Section-3 looks at province-based work. The experience described in this section is a pointer, firstly, to the importance of looking at subnational budgets in a situation where much of the spending occurs in these decentralised units. Secondly, the particular experience described here shows both the possibilities and difficulties of working with legislatures. Finally, section 4 looks at revenue. Again, we include this because it is an under-explored aspect of gender budget work. Further, even where countries have looked at revenue, the analysis has usually been confined to taxation.

Development of Workshop Materials

Why produce workshop materials?

The first concrete product of the South African WBI was a book containing the analysis of a selection of sectoral budgets, public sector employment and taxation. *The Women's Budget* (Budlender, ed., 1996) contained seven chapters. Authors were asked to keep their chapters to a maximum of thirty pages in simple, non-academic language. Editing attempted to ensure that the product was not seen as an academic, inaccessible tome. The subsequent Women's Budget books followed the same format and style.

Despite our attempts at simplicity, we suspected that few people read our research work in this form. Of those who read it, the majority were probably people with higher education, rather than the broader audience we hoped to reach. In particular, we knew that South Africa has no educational qualifications for becoming a member of parliament. We would thus be missing many of our immediate partners.

Our first attempt to remedy the situation was a set of *Money Matters* publications (see, for example, Hurt & Budlender, eds., 1998). These books took the material from the longer books, but converted each chapter into ten pages of simple English. The publication was also illustrated with photographs. In adapting the material, our target audience was someone with ten years of education whose first language was not English. In 2001, we went further and translated the *Money Matters* version of the chapter on customs and excise (see below) into three indigenous languages. This last product was disseminated through trade unions for whom customs and excise was a key issue. In particular, we targeted the clothing and textile workers' union.

Money Matters proved more popular than the *Women's Budget* series. But we still felt that we were not reaching our full potential audience. Even the shorter, simpler books had to contend with a public that had a weak reading culture and that was not in the habit of purchasing books. A far more common activity for our target audiences was attending workshops.

The process of producing the materials for South Africa

The WBI therefore teamed up with a gender training organisation, the Gender Education and Training Network (GETNET), with the express aim of producing a set of gender budget workshop materials. The partnership obtained funding from the gender project of the German technical cooperation agency (GTZ) to produce a set of materials that would help people understand the concepts, approach and findings of the WBI's work.

As with our other activities, the WBI and GETNET did not work alone on this project. We brought together a team of adult educators, materials developers and some of the researchers from the WBI. We kicked off the project with a workshop at which we decided on the topics that would need to be addressed and possible exercises. We agreed that our target audience would be people with training skills so that we would not have to cover the basics of training. We decided that we would restrict the general section on gender as there were several other workbooks from which one could obtain exercises for gender training. We were anxious not to duplicate that work and to keep our own materials down to a manageable size.

The work was divided up between participants, who after the workshop worked on their sections on their own. In a second workshop we then went through and tested some of what had been produced. After a final editing process, we advertised for organisations prepared to test some of the materials and provide feedback. We made some further changes on the basis of the feedback and produced the final product. Each participant received a small payment for participating in the workshop and work done afterwards, but most of the work was unpaid.

The final product, which we also called *Money Matters*, took the form of a folder divided into three modules. These modules were further sub-divided into a number of sessions. Each session contained the objectives of the session, information as to time and materials needed, detailed instructions for each of the exercises, and all handouts required for the exercises. After some debate as to the desirability of colour coding of sections, we decided to produce everything on white paper so as to facilitate photocopying.

We saw the set of materials as a 'mix-and-match' pack. We did not expect any workshop to go through all the material. Rather, we hoped that trainers would be able to select particular sessions and exercises, and integrate them into workshops on gender, on budgets, on particular sectors, on advocacy, and so on.

The materials were expressly tailored towards a civil society audience, or one made up of public representatives. This target informed both the tone and what we covered. For example, the final module of the materials focused on advocacy. A separate manual (Budlender & Sharp, 1998), commissioned by the Commonwealth Secretariat, had government as its audience as it grew out of the Secretariat's pilot gender budget initiatives based in government. In practice, however, sections of the *Money Matters* workshop materials have been used in training civil servants both in South Africa and beyond.

Producing materials for the Southern African region

The materials we had produced were targeted at a South African audience. Their South African-ness was apparent in virtually all sessions, but more evident in some than others. For example, the sessions on gender made reference to the South African constitution's emphasis on equality; the sessions on parliament described the composition and functioning of the national and provincial legislatures; the sessions on the budget process described the different bodies included in the process; the sessions on intergovernmental relations described the functions of national, provincial and local government and how money flowed between them; and the session on advocacy used examples of past struggles in the country.

Despite the South African focus, many exercises worked well when used in other countries, although in most cases at least some adaptation was necessary. As it became evident that the international interest in gender budget work was unlikely to diminish in the short term, GETNET and WBI had the idea of working together with others in the Southern African Development Community (SADC) to produce a set of materials adapted for the different country situations.

Although several potential donors were keen that we work with all countries in the region, we decided that, as this was an experiment and because we had limited capacity because of other work, we should begin with a subset of SADC countries. We chose countries where we had contacts or where we knew that gender budget work had already begun. Our target countries at the start of the initiative were thus Botswana, Mozambique, Namibia, Zambia and Zimbabwe. The UNIFEM regional office in Harare agreed to fund the work.

We invited two researchers from each of the countries to a three-day workshop in Cape Town. Before the workshop we went through the materials and identified the exercises and handouts which might need adaptation. The full set of materials, together with this list, was sent to each team of researchers. Their 'homework' before the workshop was to attempt to collect the relevant information.

The process did not go as smoothly as we had hoped. Firstly, not all the teams did the homework. At least one reason was that we did not recognise the extent to which participants would need background information and understanding of gender budget work to be able to undertake the task. Secondly, by selecting only researchers for this workshop, we underestimated the extent to which an understanding of adult education, training and materials development was necessary. Thirdly, we assumed that participants would be prepared to do the work for the same minimal payments as the South Africans had done. This assumption was not correct in respect of everyone.

In planning the workshop, we had foreseen that we would use it to work further on the homework, and that participants would then return home to fill in missing information. We proceeded with this plan, even though it was clear that for most countries the work would involve much more than filling in a little bit of information. Because of our mistakes in planning described above, among other reasons, only two countries completed the second set of homework, namely Botswana and Zimbabwe. We decided that it was better to continue with a smaller set of countries that had real interest, than a larger group which included some with less commitment.

For the second workshop, we asked the original researchers to bring with them four or five additional people from their country. We asked that these be people with experience in training and materials development, and who would be likely to use the materials. With this changed composition, the second workshop proceeded far more smoothly than the first one.

The job was, however, still not finished. The country participants were again sent back with specific tasks in respect of finding missing information and developing country-appropriate handouts for the different exercises. This process took much longer than expected as participants were dispersed across different organisations and all were again occupied with their ordinary work. The work is finally complete, however, and UNIFEM has undertaken to publish and disseminate the product.

Violence Against Women

Violence against women crosses the divides

The WBI has consistently emphasised that gender is not the only axis of disadvantage in either South Africa or any other country. In particular, in South Africa race continues to be an important determinant of an individual's situation and prospects. Further important factors include location (rural and urban, province, etc), class and age. The WBI focused on issues affecting the most disadvantaged, namely those who, in addition to being female, were black, rural and poor.

There is, however, at least one issue that affects women across class, race and other divides. That issue is violence against women. During the process leading up to the 1994 elections which ended apartheid, women united across class, race and political party in the Women's National Coalition. In this process, it became evident that opposition to violence against women could be a unifying factor. Further, statistics suggest that the prevalence of violence against women is higher in South Africa than in many other countries.

The WBI recognised the importance of gender violence in its first set of research reports. In the second year, one of the chapters focused on the budgets of the Departments of Safety and Security (police) and Justice and Correctional Services (prisons). (In South Africa, we use the word 'Department' where most countries would use 'Ministry'.) In each of these departments, the author focused her attention on what policies, programmes and budgets were being directed against gender violence.

A new act as a focus of advocacy

A few years later, the issue of budgets and gender violence was taken up by another NGO. In 1993, shortly before the elections, the last apartheid government passed a series of laws addressing gender issues. One of these was the domestic violence act. The law was a step forward, but it soon became evident that it had many weaknesses. In 1998, the post-apartheid government introduced a new domestic violence act, which improved on the previous one in a number of important ways.

It was at this stage that civil society activists started asking questions about how effectively the new law would be implemented. In particular, alerted to the importance of resources by the publicity around the WBI, they asked whether a budget had been allocated for implementation. The Minister of Justice responded by saying that two million rand had been set aside for this purpose. However, when questioned further, he could not say how this money would be used.

Concern at this lack of clarity provoked the Gender Advocacy Programme (GAP) to coordinate an information session for other NGOs in June 1998. At this session, the Community Agency for Social Enquiry (CASE), which was one of the core partners of the WBI, provided input on how the allocation of government funds happens. The exploratory session laid the basis for a further workshop in May 1999. The second workshop, hosted by GAP and facilitated by CASE, explicitly discussed the budgetary implications of the new law. The workshop brought together activists from eight NGOs that assist victims of domestic violence, deal practically with domestic violence issues as part of their daily work or have expertise in looking at budgets. After the workshop, GAP commissioned CASE to conduct research into the planned implementation of the Act and related budgets. The problem areas raised at the workshop were used as a starting point for the research.

The earlier WBI research had already pointed to the fact that a range of government departments perform functions relevant to domestic violence. To keep things manageable, it was agreed that CASE would focus on the Departments of Justice, Safety and Security and Welfare. A further complication is that some of the responsibility for implementation of the law lies with provincial rather than national government. It was agreed that CASE would use the Western Cape province as a case study. This choice would bias the findings to the extent that the Western Cape is in many ways wealthier than other provinces. However, the province had the highest per capita serious crime rate in the country. Further, GAP was based there.

The research revealed that there had, in fact, been some planning in government as to how to spend the two million rand allocation. In particular, much of the money was to be used for training civil servants responsible for the new functions specified in the law. Beyond this specific allocation, there were also other activities and allocations by departments. Nevertheless, the plans and allocations would clearly not be adequate to realise the full potential of the Act.

The concrete output of the project was a report entitled *Making the Act Work* (Goldman, 1999). GAP distributed the publication widely, both within South Africa and beyond. It also organised a dissemination workshop to which it invited national and provincial government officials and NGOs representatives concerned about gender violence. At this workshop, participants discussed the findings and recommendations. Subsequently, the Western Cape Network on Violence Against Women, which brings together NGO and government players, again took up the issue.

Researching for parliament

In 2000, the parliamentary Committee on Improvement of the Quality of Life and Status of Women (CIQLFW) decided that it would focus its attention on violence against women, alongside poverty and HIV/AIDS, as the most serious problems affecting South African women. As part of this new strategy, the committee commissioned CASE and GETNET to undertake research into the budget aspects of the three foci. The partners, in turn, commissioned the Centre for the Study of Violence and Reconciliation (CSVR) to cover the issue of violence against women. CSVR was not a women's or gender organisation, but had a strong gender unit. This unit had previously undertaken solid research into different aspects of gender violence, and was also involved in service provision and training of civil servants, particularly police. It thus had an excellent understanding of many of the issues which needed to be covered.

From its side, CSVR was keen to take forward research on government spending to combat violence against women. In addition to the parliamentary request, there were two other sources of impetus. The first was a training programme aimed at reducing the secondary victimisation of rape survivors, and the second was a South African Law Commission discussion paper exploring the feasibility of a victims' compensation fund.

Multi-pronged research and advocacy

Reducing the secondary victimisation of rape survivors

In 2000 the Gender Unit of CSVR ran a training programme aimed at reducing the secondary victimisation of rape survivors. The trainees were detectives from around the country working within the government's specialist Family Violence, Child Protection and Sexual Offences (FCS) Units. While developing the training, CSVR saw secondary victimisation as resulting from sexist stereotyping and prejudice towards rape survivors. Their solution to the problem was thus training and information to challenge such attitudes. By the end of the training, however, CSVR had a more complex understanding of the problem. They understood that under-resourcing played a significant role in the inadequate treatment of rape survivors. Indeed, the ill-treatment of women was almost guaranteed when government institutions did not adequately equip their employees with the skills, workplace support and material resources to carry out their duties effectively and compassionately. This led CSVR to the WBI as a way of exploring the gap between policy and implementation.

A victims' compensation fund?

At about the same time as CSVR started planning the research, the Law Commission released a discussion paper, *Sentencing: A Compensation Scheme for Victims of Crime in South Africa* (SA Law Commission, 2001). The report proposed that rape survivors who report their crime and cooperate with the criminal justice system be given an amount of R2,000 in compensation. The idea of compensating women for the violence done to them was an interesting one. Exactly what are the costs associated with victimisation? How does one put a value to suffering?

From these starting points, CSVR chose to focus on three different aspects of government financing of initiatives to combat violence against women:

◆ describing and analysing the nature, range and extent of government support for NGOs providing services to women experiencing gender-based violence;

◆ assessing national and provincial budgetary allocations towards the development and implementation of policies and legislation; and

◆ developing a preliminary analysis of costs of violence against women to the state, society and individuals.

The survey

In June 2001 CSVR sent out a national survey to 196 organisations around the country. Each of these organisations had been identified as offering some form of service to women aged fifteen years and older who had experienced gender-based violence. Ultimately, 142 organisations (or 72%) responded to the questionnaire. Most of the organisations were willing to provide CSVR with information about their government funding. Their responses allowed CSVR to calculate how much money government departments provided to organisations, as well as which government departments provided the most support. CSVR also learnt how few organisations were tendering for government work in the area of gender violence. They learnt, conversely, how few tenders were put out for this work.

From research to workshops

The research highlighted that the organisations' lack of knowledge about government funding and tendering processes was hampering their ability to secure this funding. As a next step CSVR developed a training programme and participants' manual aimed at increasing organisations' knowledge. The executive summary of the research report was included in the participant pack. The pack also included application forms for various funds, the Department of Social Development's service plan, and tips on tendering and proposal writing. Where possible, CSVR included contact information for the provincial government departments. The organisation invited government representatives to each workshop to explain their service plan. Unfortunately, these representatives were present at only two out of the five workshops.

Participants commented that, while they had participated in a number of research projects, this was the first time researchers had 'returned' information to them and asked for input around the research recommendations.

Interviewing government employees

This proved to be the most challenging component of the study. To assist in gaining access to information, the parliamentary committee provided CSVR at the outset with a letter confirming that it had commissioned the research. Nevertheless, some government employees still ignored telephone calls and repeated requests for information. It was easier to get women to talk about their very painful experiences of being raped, abused or infected with HIV than it was to persuade some government employees to provide information about their budgets, programmes and expenditure. However, those government employees who did make time were often extremely helpful. They provided figures for their projects, as well as insight into some of the reasons why budgets were not spent or projects were under-resourced.

One serious obstacle in this research was that government departments do not disaggregate their budgets in much detail. Overall totals for training or personnel are provided, but there is no breakdown, for example, of how many clerks around the country are specifically employed to implement the domestic violence act. In an attempt to flesh out some of this detail, CSVR undertook case studies at two courts to illustrate the resources, both human and material, needed to implement the act.

The women's study

Estimating the costs that violence imposes on the women involved is a very difficult endeavour. Most studies attempting to look at the costs of victimisation have used surveys and focused their questions on either the worst incidents of violence, or violence experienced within a particular time frame. CSVR had neither the money nor the time to conduct such a survey. They also felt that this approach would not capture the cumulative experience of repeated abuse.

Instead, CSVR chose to provide a series of case studies illustrating a diverse set of women's experiences over time. This approach illustrated the complexity of violence in women's lives. However, it did not always produce the kind of precise detail that statisticians desire. For example, women who have experienced multiple abuses can not remember the details of each incident after a while. The interviews also highlighted women's under-usage of services. This suggested that violence against women cost the state less than it should, and that women and their families were bearing the burden of the costs.

CSVR deliberately selected women from a variety of life circumstances. In doing so, they were able to show how marginalisation excludes some women more than others from South African society's benefits and leaves them to bear the brunt of the costs of victimisation.

Where to from here?

CSVR's research and follow-up activities began very soon to produce results. The frustration expressed at the workshops around the distribution policies of key government-related funding bodies led in some instances to the formation of cross-provincial task teams. These teams were to meet with the various boards and government departments – although some participants had no faith in this process and decided to address their complaints to the media.

Further, both the government and organisational survey reports can function as baseline studies against which government's progress can be measured. They also have the potential to support advocacy around future budgets.

It is not clear at this stage to what extent the parliamentary committee will use the research that CSVR conducted for them. However, by raising further funds, expanding the research focus, and building dissemination, organisation and advocacy into its strategies, CSVR avoided the danger of having a solid research effort gather dust on the shelves.

Province-based Work

South Africa has nine provinces, each of which has its own legislature, executive and budget. National government is responsible for overall policy-making, but provinces bear the main responsibility for delivery of health, education and welfare. They are thus key foci for gender budget work.

KwaZulu-Natal, on the east coast, has the largest population of all the provinces and is also one of the poorest. Gender budget work has advanced quite far in the province, largely due to the work of an NGO, the Provincial Parliamentary Programme (PPP). The PPP, as its name implies, works mainly with the provincial legislature. However, it has drawn in the other gender structures in the province as well. The box gives a brief description of the structures that make up the 'provincial gender machinery' in KwaZulu-Natal. Other provinces have similar, though not identical, structures.

The Provincial Gender Machinery

The formal gender structures in KwaZulu-Natal are as follows:

Legislature: There are 80 public representatives in the legislature, of whom 21 are women. These women members of the provincial legislature (MPLs) have formed a parliamentary women's caucus (PWC), whose function is to:

- be a forum in which MPLs discuss gender issues, and agree on a common platform;
- be a forum for capacity building of women MPLs;
- provide a central point of access for advocacy by civil society;
- provide a central point for women MPLs to communicate with women's organisations; and
- ensure that all legislation put before the legislature is gender-sensitive.

The PWC has lobbied for the creation of a provincial standing committee on women, children, youth and disabled persons, similar to the committee on women in the national parliament. The committee would be responsible for monitoring the performance of government departments and drafting legislation. To date, the committee has not been formally established.

Provincial executive: In December 2001 the provincial executive established a provincial Office on the Status of Women (OSW) within the Premier's Office. This body mirrors a similar body in the national President's office. Its task is to coordinate an inter-departmental forum of gender focal points from each of the provincial departments.

Commission on Gender Equality (CGE): This is a national body established under South Africa's constitution. Its mandate is to monitor and promote gender equality. The Commission has a provincial office in KwaZulu-Natal.

Civil society: There is no single organised gender structure within civil society, but there are many sectoral networks, of varying strength.

2001/02 budget period

In early 2001, shortly before the annual budget hearings, the PPP, PWC and provincial office of the Commission on Gender Equality (CGE) established the province's first women's budget initiative. The partners developed a document outlining what a women's budget can achieve, and the legislature's responsibility to support such an initiative. They developed a standard set of questions and asked the legislature's finance portfolio committee to give these questions to all provincial departments for written response during the budget hearings process. The PPP and PWC lobbied the then chairperson of the finance committee and got his support for the initiative. The committee included the proposed questions word-for-word in their set of questions to all departments.

The PPP reported on this achievement to a meeting of the PWC, and urged them to monitor departments' responses during the budget hearings. The PPP suggested that the answers could be used as a baseline for follow-up during the course of the year.

Out of a total of 13 provincial departments, nine included detailed responses to the gender questions. The other departments either reported that they provide equally for men and women and that women are not discriminated against, or that the questions were not relevant to their line function, or they simply ignored the gender questions. Unfortunately, the committee members did not interrogate any of the responses. Further, no-one took the initiative to compile the gender information collected through the hearings and provide this to the PWC, CGE or civil society organisations for follow-up.

2002/03 budget period

The partners to the 2001/2002 budget initiative tried again the next year, and brought the newly established provincial office of the OSW on board. The group decided on a new approach. Instead of standard questions, they developed sector-specific questions for each department.

The PWC and PPP had previously approached the new finance portfolio committee chairperson. He said he would cooperate as the committee had done the previous year. However, he later refused to send the sector-specific questions to the departments. He said they were too long and detailed for the hearings, and that the PWC should send them to departments directly.

At first the PWC delayed sending the questions to departments, as they felt this should be done by the new standing committee on women. However, after delays in establishing the committee, the PWC decided that it should submit the questions as parliamentary questions for written reply, and that the other bodies should then monitor what happened.

Training interventions

In October 2001, the PPP was asked to organise a session on gender budgeting as part of a finance workshop for portfolio committee chairpersons. The session covered:

◆ understanding the concept of a women's budget;

◆ an overview of the national WBI;

◆ gender equality and budget analysis; and

◆ introducing gender into the provincial budget process.

The fourth part drew on departmental commitments during the 2001/02 budget process and included a practical exercise. The exercise took participants through the budget process so that they could identify steps that they could take at every stage to raise gender issues.

Analysis of approach and achievements

The 2001/2 and 2002/3 activities did not achieve as much as the partners had hoped. Many of the reasons were related to weaknesses in structures:

◆ Inter-party tensions and lack of focus and capacity within the PWC prevented proper planning and coordinated, united action.

◆ An inter-departmental forum was set up in the Premier's Office prior to the establishment of the OSW. This forum was not accessible or accountable to either civil society or the provincial legislature. It was also not in an appropriate position, and did not have the organisational capacity, to monitor departmental budgets itself.

◆ The provincial OSW was struggling to establish itself. It had the status of a sub-directorate, and had been allocated inadequate resources for its mandate.

◆ The CGE had limited resources. One full-time and one part-time commissioner served both KwaZulu-Natal and another province, and the office had limited management and support staff.

◆ There was no organised civil society gender structure to take up issues of gender budgeting.

The 2001/2 approach, in the form of a set of standard questions to departments, was successful in that the finance portfolio committee used their muscle to get responses from departments. But the MPLs did not actively scrutinise departmental budgets during the budget hearings. They also did not monitor the implementation of the budget. The initiative did, however, identify the need for a provincial women's

167

budget initiative. It also forged strong links between the PWC, CGE and PPP around the issue.

The 2002/3 approach, in seeking more detailed information from departments, alienated the finance portfolio committee. This left the initiative in the hands of the PWC. The alliance was strengthened with the bringing on board of the provincial OSW. It should be further strengthened in the near future by the formation of the joint standing committee.

Looking at Revenue

Most gender budget initiatives have focused their attention on expenditure rather than revenue. This is understandable and sensible in developing countries, where a large proportion of the resources are external. Nevertheless, revenue is an important issue. In terms of process, when governments draw up budgets, the first step is usually to determine the resource envelope, i.e. to determine levels and sources of revenue. Expenditure must then be planned within this envelope. Further, taxation – and particularly direct taxation – is not the only form of revenue that is open to gender analysis.

The WBI from the start recognised the importance of revenue. The first round of research included a chapter on taxation. The chapter looked at gender and poverty issues in both direct and indirect taxation. The fourth round of research included a chapter on donor funds. This research was based primarily on structured interviews with representatives of the thirty-odd bilateral and multilateral donors who together contributed about 2 per cent of the national budget.

In the fifth year of the initiative, revenue became the centre of attention. Three papers were produced: an update on taxation, an analysis of customs and excise, and an investigation of gender issues in local government revenue.

Customs and excise was a completely new area for the initiative. In tackling the topic, the researcher was able to draw on the work and experience of affected trade unions and, in particular, the Southern African Clothing and Textile Workers Union (SACTWU). She was also able to draw on the international literature on gender and trade. As noted above, the resulting chapter in *Money Matters* was translated into three indigenous languages and distributed to trade unions.

To date, however, the gender aspects of revenue have not really been taken up. From the media it is clear that, for the upper and middle classes, the taxation aspect of revenue is of key interest in every budget. When the budget speech is delivered, there is also great interest in what the Minister of Finance will announce in respect of 'sin' taxes on alcohol and tobacco. Among poorer people and their advocates, however, the focus is still on expenditure. It is thus more difficult to find groups to take the research forward into advocacy.

Conclusion

This chapter has looked at a range of ways in which South African work in the gender budget field has expanded in terms of focus, approach and players. As noted, the approach is more widespread in South Africa than in many other countries.

Nevertheless, the majority of South Africans would still be perplexed if they heard the term 'gender budget'. Further, at this stage there is very little activity inside government. In the late 1990s the national Department of Finance had a gender budget initiative for two years as part of the broader Commonwealth Secretariat pilot initiative. In those years the standard publications tabled on budget day included discussion of gender issues. About two years ago, one of the provinces instituted a gender budget initiative. Top officials of each of the eight provincial departments were trained and produced detailed gender budget statements. At the last moment, however, the person responsible for producing the budget documents omitted these pieces.

When asked recently about the disappearance of gender budget work within government, a top official in the Treasury responded that they were "doing it". Correctly, he saw the gender budget as focusing on how government was addressing the needs and interests of disadvantaged people, including women. What he failed to see, however, was the need to disaggregate disadvantage, so as to understand the ways in which needs and interests differ. What he also failed to see was the need for government to be transparent in the way it reports what it is doing. In particular, the government's move towards a programme approach in budgeting requires it to develop targets and indicators of delivery alongside figures saying how many rands it has allocated and spent. To date, however, the targets and indicators are poorly developed in general terms, let alone in terms of gender disaggregation.

References

Budlender D. (ed). (1996). *The Women's Budget.* Institute for Democracy in South Africa, Cape Town.

Budlender D. (2000). "The Political Economy of Women's Budgets in the South" in *World Development* 28(7), July: 1365–1378.

_____ and R. Sharp with K. Allen (1998). *How to do a gender-sensitive budget analysis: Contemporary research and practice.* AusAID and Commonwealth Secretariat, Canberra and London.

Goldman T. (1999). *Making the Act Work: A research study into the budget allocations for the implementation of the domestic violence act.* Gender Advocacy Programme, Cape Town.

Hurt K. and D. Budlender (eds). (1998). *Money Matters: Women and the Government Budget.* Institute for Democracy in South Africa, Cape Town.

South African Law Commission (2001). *Sentencing: A Compensation Scheme for Victims of Crime in South Africa.* Discussion Paper 97 of Project 82, Pretoria

United Kingdom: A Focus on taxes and benefits

Donna St. Hill

Table 14: Selected Indicators for the UK

Indicator	*Year*	*Number*
Population	2000	59.8
% of population which is female	2001	51%
% of population which is urban (England & Wales)	2001	79%
Gross domestic product (GDP) per capita (US$)	1999	22,897
Human development index (HDI)	1999	0.923
Gender development index (GDI)	1999	0.920
% of total budget funded by donors	2002	0%
% of national parliamentarians who are women	2001	17.9%

Introduction

The Women's Budget Group (WBG) in the United Kingdom (UK) refers to itself as a think tank on the relationship between women, men and economics. It brings together independent feminists, economists and social policy experts with others from a range of equality-seeking non-governmental organisations (NGOs), unions and research organisations. Members represent their own views, which are informed by their specialist work as researchers on gender and social policy, as trade unionists and as public economists, as well as by their and their organisation's experience in the field of advocacy and public policy.

The work and the achievements of the WBG have reached a new prominence since the coming to power of a New Labour government in 1997. The change from Conservative to the centre-left political administration of the New Labour Party facilitated not only a more sympathetic political directorate in Westminster, but also what appears to be a more genuinely open agenda, including paying attention to the voices of women.

Because of this, the fortunes of New Labour and the WBG have so far been positively intertwined. Listening to women's representatives is part of a general policy of the UK Government to consult more widely with stakeholders prior to formulating policy. As a result, the WBG has expanded its advocacy capabilities from commenting on the budget after it is released to engaging in a two-way dialogue with Treasury before the budget is developed. It has also engaged throughout the year-in a range of gender-relevant policy issues with a small number of key government departments, such as Social Security, Work and Pensions and the Inland Revenue.

The institutional capacity of the WBG was greatly enhanced in the fall of 1999 with the grant from the Barrow Cadbury Trust to fund the salary of a part-time project manager. At that time Oxfam's UK Poverty Programme provided an additional grant to finance publishing and special projects should the need arise. The human resource boost enabled a more sustained outreach and a fuller programme of official activities among key government departments as well as the coordination of the voluntary labour of WBG members and interns to prepare for and participate in government meetings. The extra, dedicated resources on a consistent basis also led to the launch of the WBG's first website, the establishment of a media presence, and a significant expansion of membership.

This chapter traces the issues and opportunities facing the development of the WBG in the UK and its work to make economic policy making reflect women's perspectives and priorities. The first section looks at its history, paying particular attention to how different governing philosophies of government administrations have influenced the nature of gender budgeting in the UK. The following section examines the current budgetary process in the UK and the ways in which the WBG has been able to utilise particular administrative and political changes as useful leverage for persuading government to deliver on the gender agenda. The strengths and subsequent successes of the WBG's experience are discussed in the next two sections. After an assessment of some of the practical and strategic challenges at the present stage of development, the chapter concludes with a brief look at some of the future opportunities for promoting gender budgeting within the UK.

History of the WBG

The WBG was established in 1989 when a number of feminist women, mainly academics, got together to discuss the implications of the relationship between gender relations and macro economic policy. In the course of its development, a few men have expressed interest in membership, but their contributions have so far been limited.

For the first eight years of WBG's existence, members met as an informal group to comment on the UK budget on an annual basis. However, throughout this period the Conservative government then in power did not see the need to entertain its critique of budgetary policies. The WBG therefore found itself producing commentaries on the budgets after they were announced with no acknowledgement from government. Media attention was also minimal despite an invitation in one year from the British Broadcasting Corporation (BBC) to be part of its live commentary of the budget. Overall, during the Conservative years, WBG's main work with politicians involved providing briefing papers for opposition parties to criticise successive government budgets.

With the change of government to New Labour in 1997, both the extent and the form of engagement with the budgetary process changed dramatically. Some months after the general election, and with the help of the Cabinet Office's Women and Equality Unit (WEU), the WBG attended its first exploratory meeting with the Treasury. The WBG now has regular meetings with the Treasury. It meets pre- and post-budget, but also in a series of policy seminars and roundtable meetings on a range of policy issues, some of which it introduces.

Recently, the WBG has cemented functional linkages with the Cabinet Office through the WEU and the Women's National Commission (WNC) by collaborating in, and often leading, intellectual arguments for policy changes on a number of longstanding women's issues. The WEU is the UK Government's unit for commissioning and assembling research and data on women. The WNC, which is also in the Cabinet Office, is an agency set up by the government to give women a voice in Westminster. The issues collaborated on include the importance of a policy focus on the individual as well as on the household or family; consideration of the long-term gender effects of policy; the incorporation of the unpaid, care economy in national accounting systems; closing the gender, productivity and pay gaps; and the differential responses between men and women to economic incentives.

These relationships with the Cabinet Office have proved invaluable for raising the WBG's profile and gaining access to high-ranking government officials. They have also resulted in an enhancement of the specialist capacity of women-focused state units such as the WEU and the WNC in the areas of gender analysis and economic literacy for female empowerment.

The WBG has benefited especially from its close links with the WNC. The relationship has provided it with considerable access to senior government officials, including government ministers, for private meetings and consultations. It is also of significant value that the Director of the WNC is committed to the ideals of the Group and is exceptionally well versed in political diplomacy and the policy-making processes within government. In the beginning, meetings with government officials occurred only after the WNC Director had written letters or made phone calls to senior civil service colleagues introducing the idea of gender analysis and explaining how this might benefit their different policy agendas. Now, however, policy makers keen on examining how a gender perspective on their policy formulations would be beneficial are approaching the WBG at a faster rate than the Group's existing capacity to respond effectively.

However, while being an independent body that is able to scrutinise policy for unacknowledged gender effects has its advantages, there are also substantial limitations to how far the WBG can go, as an external organisation, in taking forward gender budget work. This is an issue we will return to later.

In October 2001, with a new public profile in Westminster, greater awareness of its activities nationally and internationally, and a growing media presence creating heightened expectations, the WBG met to reconsider its strategic future. At the end of the meeting the Group had its first formalised, multi-part description of itself. In particular, the document stated that the aims and goals of the WBG were to:

◆ develop analysis and lead debate on the gender implications of economic policy, bearing in mind the multiple dimensions of women's disadvantage;

◆ expand understanding among policy makers and opinion formers of the gender implications of economic policy and give policy advice;

◆ promote gender mainstreaming in economic policy making, presentation and monitoring; and

◆ work with other organisations to raise public awareness of gender equality issues in economic policy and the importance of assessing the effects of economic policy on women.

The Budgetary Process in the UK

An annual statement of taxes and benefits

The budgetary process in the UK is somewhat different from other countries and this has shaped the nature of the WBG's relationship with the Treasury. It influences both the range of issues on which the WBG engages the government and also the focus of discussions.

Within the UK budgetary process, there is a biennial Spending Review which sets government spending for the departments for the next budgetary year along with projected spending for the following three budgetary years. In these aspects the process is similar to that in other countries. However, the UK budget itself is the annual statement of changes in taxes and benefits and the regulations relating to them, rather than the statement on revenue and expenditures common in other countries. On Budget day the Chancellor concentrates on revenue-raising measures and only broadly outlines departmental expenditure plans. In the days following the Spending Review, individual departments announce the details of spending and policy reforms, usually in media conferences.

The WBG has concentrated on taxes and benefits rather than the specific gendered effects of government expenditure as most other gender budget initiatives do. However, it is encouraging the government to commit itself to this annual exercise on all forms of taxation as well as expenditure. This is an area that will require more lobbying in order to move from a situation in which government invites critical gender analysis to where it performs this function itself.

A practical reason why the WBG has focused its efforts on taxes and benefits is that there are fewer of them than there are spending programmes. Further, many of the taxes and benefits apply to individuals, making gender effects more easily identifiable (Himmelweit, 2000: 6). However, while even small changes to these policies may end up having a huge impact on a government's entire economic strategy, they are notoriously difficult to lobby on. The difficulties arise principally because of entrenched gender assumptions that underpin economic analysis. Challenging these means putting the analytical spotlight on precisely those areas which economists have been trained not to see. Accepting the full implications of gender analysis for economic policy is therefore inherently revolutionary for economists as well as for the women who will come into contact with truly engendered policy reform. The fact that tax and benefit instruments can be bearers of profound gender bias only becomes clear when analysts expose the philosophical principles at work in the relationship between one tax and another. Welfare to work policies that contain inadequate or no child-care provision, the payment of tax incentives and benefits to the sole earner in households on the assumption of joint use of family income, and state benefit systems that rely on the 'typical' or 'normal' working life are some examples of these systemic gender biases.

Key principles for assessing gender impact

In terms of methodology, the WBG has advised the government to employ five key principles in assessing the impact of budgetary measures.

1. Analytical attention needs to be paid to both the individual and the family. If gender effects are to be seen clearly and factored into policy planning, it is essential to understand the distinct impacts of budgets at the individual and household level.

2. The long-term effects of policy need to be considered. Some of the most important goals of government policy relate to human development and balancing the division of paid and unpaid work between states, communities and families. These involve social transformations that take place slowly over decades, perhaps even generations. Therefore, policy designed today must consider its impact on the achievement of valued long-term societal goals with a view to making short-term changes supportive of long-term stability and goals.

3. Analysis needs to be extended to factors such as employment, poverty, education and the unpaid, care economy. The continuing impact of unpaid care work on women's employment, poverty rates and participation in all forms of public life must be addressed

by policy makers if they are to realise the full potential of policy reform in these areas.

4. It needs to be understood that men and women's different and unequal positioning gives rise to different, gendered responses to economic incentives. Simplistic models of economic behaviour need to be replaced by more sophisticated modelling that takes into account the trade-offs between paid and unpaid work and the opportunity costs for men and women of participating in each sphere.

5. Finally, the ways in which policy challenges or entrenches gender stereotypes need careful examination. Measures to foster interchangeable practices between men and women's participation in paid work and the unpaid care economy is central not only to the economic potential of women, but also to the full human development of men.

Recommended methods for gender analysis

There are a number of ways in which government can be advised to carry out gender analysis as part of its budgetary process. The table below outlines five methods that the WBG advocates for inserting gender analysis into the budget. The methods range from fairly simple to more complex techniques.

Table 15: Tools for introducing gender analysis into the UK budgetary process

	Questions explored	*Requirements*
1. Making gender visible	Who are the recipients?	Data disaggregated by sex
2. Auditing revenue and expenditure	How is spending/revenue distributed between women and men?	Expenditure and revenue statistics disaggregated by sex
3. Gender impact assessment	What are implications in the short and long term for the gender distribution of: – resources (money and time)? – paid and unpaid work?	Data on the unpaid, caring economy, for example, a satellite account incorporating time use data

	Is provision adequate to the needs of women and men?	Micro-analytic model of income distribution, incorporating model of economic (e.g. labour supply) and other (e.g. fertility) behaviour sensitive to gender differentials
	How does policy affect gender norms and roles?	
		Sensitivity to gender segregation, cultural practices and gender norms and the impact that policy has on supporting or reconstructing these.
4. Gender mainstreaming	How is gender taken into account in policy formulation, design and implementation?	Cooperation across government agencies and across the policy process
	What priorities are given to reducing gender inequality?	Awareness of the scope of gender issues and ability to search out more hidden aspects of gender inequality
		Tools to assess the aims and priorities attached to policy
5. Benchmarking	Are specific targets for gender equality being met?	Awareness of complexity of gender inequalities when setting targets Ability to locate the policy and other influences on particular social phenomena

Source: Rake, 2002: 10

The first method requires a statistical reckoning of the numbers of men and women affected by a particular policy. This depends on the availability of national data sets disaggregated by gender. Making this exercise more meaningful requires gender analysis of men's and women's status and needs as well as the ways in which the policy will affect economic behaviour over the long-term.

The second level of analysis is an audit of the incidence of revenue and expenditure. The value of this exercise lies in revealing any systemic bias in policy design that results in one gender bearing an inequitably disproportionate burden or benefit from the policy. To demonstrate this point, the WBG carried out a gender analysis of one of government's flagship programmes for getting people off welfare and into work. The analysis of the New Deal programmes showed the ways in which budgetary allocations for females were significantly below those utilised by males because of erroneous and unquestioned assumptions about the needs and preferences of women and men. The argument highlighted the ways in which the assumptions of male breadwinners and stable families ran through the New Deal policies. The result was a further expansion of gender gaps between the unemployed as policy failed to keep pace with the changes in women's and men's lives. The critique also offered concrete proposals for reform in a wide range of areas. These included getting rid of the disincentive for second earners and lessening the length of unemployment required for eligibility.

The patterns of resource allocation that benefit-incidence data throw up can reveal government priorities and the emphasis government places on men or women's equitable participation in the economy. This is what is entailed in the third approach of gender impact assessment. The real issue is not just how much money is spent on women in pension and social assistance benefits (or how much taxed from men), but whether or not spending matches women's and men's needs. This requires that policy makers operate with a more sophisticated understanding of the implications of gender differentials for policy in order to conduct a gender analysis of the budget. To truly understand the implications of the data requires even more sophisticated data and analysis. For instance, the availability of time use data for the development of a satellite account of unpaid work is extremely useful in assessing the impact of the budget on the unpaid, care sector.

One well-known example of the potential misreading of government expenditure occurs in the health sector, where females consume by far the largest amount of resources. A straight reading of the numbers seems to support the thesis of male marginalisation. The issue is, however, clearly not so simple as women have more, and often different, needs from men given, in particular, their reproductive role. The absence of a health economist in the WBG has been the main reason why this issue has not been taken on in more targeted way. However, WBG members use this example in other non-health related discussions with ministers and officials, because health is probably the most glaring case of false conclusions being reached on the basis of sex-disaggregated data.

Gender mainstreaming is the next approach. Rather than a form of analysis, gender mainstreaming represents a broader set of activities with a broader set of goals. Gender mainstreaming refers to the implementation of a gender-sensitive perspective throughout the policy process and in all policy areas. The implementation of gender mainstreaming throughout the entire government machinery is an indication of an acceptance that gender analysis is not just a responsibility for women's or gender machineries, but rather that gender equality is a priority for government as a whole. Although one of the most readily grasped concepts, gender mainstreaming is turning out to be one of the most often cited works-in-progress but least implemented types of gender-sensitive bureaucratic practice.

Prior to the 2001 restructuring, the Women's Unit had the responsibility, through its championing government minister, for implementing the gender mainstreaming project throughout central government. During that period, the Women's Unit worked closely with the WBG on delivering on this central mandate. With the 2001 cabinet changes and restructuring of the former Women's Unit to the new WEU, this task no longer rests with the WEU's cabinet minister. It has now become diffused as a task of all government ministers. The absence of direct ministerial accountability and the loss of a dedicated unit within government to push the process through Westminster, combined with varying levels of understanding of the project among government departments, makes this a crucial area on which the WBG will need to think creatively. For now, it is raising the issue of gender mainstreaming with the small number of individual government departments with whom it has regular contact on other policy concerns.

The fifth type of analysis is benchmarking, which may also be incorporated into any of the previous four methodologies. Benchmarking establishes a minimum standard and a time frame over which it can realistically be achieved. In benchmarking for poverty, for example, it is necessary to enquire about specific targets for women as well as for groups of women who are additionally deprived, such as old age pensioners and ethnic minority women. The UK government has already set itself some benchmarks, for example in the area of women's participation in public life. However, in the areas in which the WBG is most interested, the government continues to listen to, but not to act on, the Group's regular call for benchmarks for reducing the pay gap, for the productivity gap and for the development of a national child-care strategy.

Separating out the various methods for carrying out gender analysis helps in achieving clarity on the division between activities which can be spearheaded by external groups like the WBG and those which are the exclusive terrain of governments. For example, only governments can implement gender mainstreaming across the public sector, even though external groups can create pressure by monitoring progress and outcomes.

Strengths of the WBG

The strengths of the WBG are in some ways unique among gender-responsive budget (GRB) initiatives. The dominance of professional economists who can speak to public sector officials in economistic language is a definite advantage that sets the WBG's work apart from most other initiatives. There is also a cadre of feminist social policy analysts and gender experts from unions, research institutions and other independent equality-seeking organisations who can translate difficult concepts into the pragmatic, jargon-filled language of 'public sector speak'. The current administration's emphasis on evidence-based policy analysis makes it more welcoming of the research and scholarly orientation of the WBG than previous governments. The fact that gender budgeting, and to some extent gender analysis, are new areas to policy makers, puts the WBG, as the leading practitioner in the field in England, at a substantial advantage.

In targeting its slim resources at the Treasury, the central government organ responsible for macroeconomic planning, the WBG has been able to build up a close working relationship with senior Treasury officials and ministers. This relationship might not have been as strong if the Group had attempted to influence government through many departments at once. The close relationship has meant that the WBG has also been able to fine-tune its strategy over time, due to increasing familiarity with Treasury officials' ways of working. It has thus concentrated its efforts on engendering the Treasury's policy agenda by using the government's willingness to take on the instrumental ways in which gender analysis could improve the efficiency of its already stated polices.

The value of the presence of a large body of knowledgeable, committed feminists who are ready to give freely of their expertise and time to the WBG's work cannot be underestimated. The fact that they provide these skills largely at their own expense is a factor not recognised by government departments who benefit from their advice. However, paid or unpaid, the WBG appears highly valued by government officials, especially by those in the Treasury, if the level of contact and consultation is anything to go by.

Successes Achieved by the WBG

After several years of irregular contact and reactive annual responses to the Pre Budget Report, which is an advance statement of the government's budgetary intentions, the WBG now enjoys privileged, sustained access to Treasury officials. This access to the research, analysis and policy-making process within the Treasury provides the space for a pro-active series of seminars and workshops that explicitly take gender perspectives into account. The shift is in large part due to the stance of Tony Blair's New Labour government.

The new currency of women's equality in political circles is greatly facilitated by New Labour's modernisation agenda for government in which policy reform, emphasising greater participation, transparency and accountability, plays a major role. This emphasis on consulting with policy communities outside government is useful for the WBG's engagement. However, there are some concerns among social activists that this appearance of openness may actually conceal the more important continuities where policy decisions are, in the main, still made by a policy elite with its own pre-determined agenda. The WBG is very aware of this possibility even while it capitalises on the Blair government's new practice of participatory government. As former Chair of the WBG, Sue Himmelweit, puts it, there is a danger that the WBG's advice could be used to pre-empt criticism by improving presentation alone rather than having any substantive gender equality impact on policy itself (Himmelwiet, 2000: 4).

The government's commitment to greater participation and transparency in its policy-making process has allowed pressure groups other than the WBG to access the budgetary process for the first time.

This has created opportunities to work with, and to some extent influence, other social policy lobbying organisations it would not ordinarily have come into contact with.

Because of the new openness within government around public consultation, the budgetary calendar has been changed. Since 1997, in addition to the opportunity offered by the Pre Budget Report to critique the government statement of intent, there is now also a longer window period in which to see ministers and officials as well as collaborate with like-minded NGOs. This budget deliberation period has allowed the WBG to collaborate more closely with trade unions, poverty action groups and pensions activists to reinforce the positions that the Group will champion. So far, there have been no major conflicts of interest. On the contrary, there has been a lot of sharing of research and coalition building with other organisations such as the leading trade unions.

In 2001 the WBG become involved for the first time in the important negotiations that preceded the Treasury-led Government Spending Review of summer 2002. This review sets out the government's spending aims for the next three years. The involvement of the Group is important. Budget day is met each year with enormous public and media attention while little attention is usually paid to the 'spending round' when it is announced later in the year. However, because governments tend to put money where their priorities are, the adoption of at least a limited gender analysis in parts of the Spending Review can have far-reaching implications for women where cuts have been suggested.

Since the 1997 election the WBG has been able to capture and hold the attention of economic planners by adopting an instrumental approach to getting gender analysis into the Treasury's ways of working. It has done this by developing a gender analysis of government's stated overriding objectives, such as raising labour force productivity, reducing child poverty and reducing welfare rolls by getting 'workless households' into work. In so doing, it is among the few advocacy groups in the UK that can advance an economic argument about efficiency of spending through the incorporation of equality analysis. There is currently no other equality lobbying or advocacy group in Britain which has successfully put an economic case for its interests before government in this way. As such, the WBG is uniquely positioned to advance economic arguments for equality more generally.

The WBG has some successes to show for its work. A major policy win, announced by Chancellor Gordon Brown in the March 2002 Budget, is that from 2003 the new Child Tax Credit (CTC) will be paid to the main carer, who is almost always a woman, rather than to the main earner, who is almost always a man. The use of efficiency grounds for transferring income from the male 'wallet' to the female 'purse' was successful because the Treasury accepted the WBG's evidence that money under women's control had a greater positive influence on child well-being and therefore on the reduction of child poverty, an important government goal. There is a danger, however, in the fact that this policy change was primarily influenced by evidence of the value of this shift in household finances for children, rather than on equity grounds for women.

After more than a decade of public obscurity, the momentum achieved with UK gender budgeting initiatives since 2000 has resulted in a heightened media presence. The WBG's official response to the Pre Budget Report of November 2000 was carried in national newspapers, including the highly regarded *Financial Times*. There was also a television interview and several follow-up radio backgrounders and newspaper quotes from the Group's budget night news release.

This media interest may have also translated into greater awareness of the WBG's work within other central government departments with whom it has had no direct contact, and among women's equality actors more generally, as there has been a sudden upsurge in requests for WBG input as speakers, seminar participants and in public sector consultations. The awareness of the WBG's work among audiences other than the Treasury, especially women's groups, is important as media engagements are one of the few ways that the Group is able to communicate gender budgeting arguments to women's leaders and grassroots activists without incurring huge communication costs.

Continuing Challenges

Overcoming the limitations of the UK's parliamentary system

While establishing close relationships with a handful of key government departments has facilitated a more meaningful, constructive engagement, the overall party political context has meant that the WBG is sometimes unable to take a sufficiently critical stance in the public arena. The cordial working relationship between the WBG and the present government can be traced back to the Group's collaboration with New Labour when it was the official opposition. Throughout that early relationship, left-leaning New Labour shadow ministers and Members of Parliament (MPs) found the WBG critique of right-wing Conservative policies to be invaluable in the party's efforts to prove the Tories were out of touch with the British people.

Much of that history still characterises the WBG/New Labour relationship today. The problem which arises is a common one in the transition from opposition to government, namely that parties are more suggestible to radical, new ideas before coming into political office than during incumbency. On the other hand, there are very few Conservative MPs who are willing to support even the most basic WBG principles publicly. It is thus no longer able to mobilise opposition support in its efforts to influence government. This dilemma is perhaps a limitation of the British parliamentary system, in which the two main parties occupy opposite ideological positions on women's empowerment, but with insufficient, organised internal cleavages, especially among the Conservatives, to allow the WBG to continue to gain political capital by exploiting political differences.

Involving more women in macroecomic processes

The status quo in Britain remains that women are largely absent from macroeconomic policy discussions. The fact that the WBG is not yet engaging in a two-way dialogue with grassroots women's NGOs presents an obstacle to widespread participation in, and scrutiny of, the macroeconomic processes by women more generally. At present the policy dialogue occurs primarily among industry specialists and government gender equality officials rather than among and on behalf of a variety of women's interests. The WBG has, however, maintained a close relationship with its equivalent number in Scotland, Engender Women's Budget Group (EWBG), which is somewhat more expansive in the constitution of its membership.

Much of the explanation for the limited engagement with wider groupings of women lies in the WBG's origins and composition, in that it has drawn heavily from academic and other research and policy environments. But it also has to do with a shortage of time and money to engage productively with women's groups around the country. The lack of engagement is becoming more and more untenable as funders begin to demand that its ways of working both reflect the participation of grassroots women's movements as well as produce outcomes that are of practical use to women's organisation working at the local levels in communities, neighbourhoods and sectors. It may take some time for the WBG's membership to view the political participation concerns of funders as central. However, the issue is one to which the WBG management committee is already responding positively.

Beyond the women's organisations generally, there is another group of women whose needs are not prioritised within the WBG's work. However, in this case there is no compelling external pressure to include their interests. Black and Asian women's gender equality politics are overwhelmingly concentrated in grassroots and informal organisations. As such they view their daily struggles against racist and sexist local institutions in Britain as the beginning and end of their organising. Yet when viewed through a gendered lens on macroeconomics, their experiences put them at the sharp end of almost all the issues the WBG wants government to take seriously in terms of policy reforms to speed up gender equality.

Beyond the WBG, the neglect of ethnic minority women's economic interests has been a longstanding feature of the male-dominated government Commission for Racial Equality (CRE) and other ethnic minority pressure groups. Because their issues are taken seriously by neither the official state gender and race equality organisations, nor the prominent non-governmental women's equality organisations, black and Asian women find they have neither a say nor a place in macroeconomic policy-making. Yet the statistics on their gendered experiences of poverty, unemployment, underemployment, harassment, low pay and work-life balance (CRE, 2001) suggest black and Asian women are urgent priorities for both the gender equality and race equality mandates at the national level. It is difficult to say whether, without pressure from funders, the WBG will interpret black and Asian's women's interests as among the ones for which they can effectively lobby government.

Taking a less academic approach to lobbying

A weakness arising from the dominance of academics in the WBG is that the policy implications arising from their gender analysis may be rigorous but are not always politically astute. This is demonstrated by the fact that, although most of its successes have been as a result of an instrumental use of gender analysis, it has been unable as yet to come up with creative ways to lead and shape the policy agenda in women's interests. One example is in getting the CTC paid to mothers on the grounds that the transfer of income to women's control would facilitate the government's stated goal of reducing child poverty rather than on grounds of gender equity. The achievement of particular outcomes in policy reform needs to be assessed against the 'why' as well as the 'what' of the reform achieved. If the feminist intent of the 'why' in policy change has been side-stepped, this can have long-term negative effects for women.

This is not to deny that many women's movements world-wide have found that instrumentalism is a useful tactic for getting policies reformed in women's favour as an *initial* strategy. However, the next part of the strategy, the subversion of entrenched gender bias among government planners by introducing normative gender analysis, is the phase that the WBG, like many feminist advocates elsewhere, struggles with (Rake, 2002: 15).

Another limitation of an academic orientation to lobbying is that many policy makers regard academics as pursuing 'ivory tower' agendas that are out of touch with the electorate of either sex. Thus, while their university and research backgrounds put the WBG in a good position technically to argue cogently for policy reforms in a way that many women's representatives would be unable to, this very strength poses limitations to the wholehearted embrace of gender reforms advocated by the Group among politicians and UK women more generally. The WBG therefore has to contend with both the common-sense scepticism of gender experts on the part of some policy elites inside government as detached theoreticians with little real-world experience, and more general anti-intellectual sentiments coming from some parts of the gender equality movement.

These problems – of non-engagement with grassroots women's groups, lobbying on white-dominated political-economic interests, and academic dominance – all have an organisational genesis. Rather than being the result of considered action on the part of the WBG, it is more plausible that they emerge from institutional constraints and inertia. Nevertheless, the fact that the WBG is seen as speaking to government for 'women', while most of the Group's constituents are not in a position to do so themselves, presents an issue of accountability since the mainly word-of-mouth membership recruitment tends to replicate the existing profile. Recently, the WBG has been revisiting its organisational strategy in light of its growing public visibility and the acknowledgement of an absence of democratic accountability in the constitution of its leadership, membership and the priorities it takes up with government on women's behalf. The strategy planning exercise in 2001 has already identified ways of surmounting some of these challenges and initiatives should soon be in place to address them.

Accessing increased funding

Funding is a more concrete limitation for the WBG. However, as we have noted, it has managed to gain a degree of access to policy makers that belies its institutional capacity. Although money has been scarce, it has managed to sustain an impressive programme of work and influence which reflects the goodwill earned in recent years. Regular activities include meetings with government ministers and officials, a series of parliamentary seminars, policy seminars for Treasury officials, and a host of official responses to government requests for consultation, among other activities. This is largely possible because the central players, as well as staff, contribute generously in unpaid labour when extra resources are required. There is an irony in the fact that it is only through almost unlimited supplies of feminists' unpaid work that an appreciation of the value of women's labour is slowing being recognised by Treasury officials, even if they have not yet started to reflect this awareness in economic policy across the board.

In light of this, there has been some consideration within the WBG of offsetting members' direct costs of lobbying – travel, publication and presentation materials – by charging government departments for expenses incurred. However, the outcome of this debate is, as yet, inconclusive. Expanding its base of core and project funders is a more readily agreed route to increasing its financial resources that the WBG has been actively pursuing since 2001.

Moving from words to action

The institutional strengths and challenges discussed so far have been ones that arise as a result of the particular origins, constitution, and feminist evolution of the WBG. However, the main challenges facing its work are likely to be identical to those faced by the women's movement internationally. The Group has been unable as yet to have a significant influence in getting government departments to move any closer to gender mainstreaming than what is called in the UK a 'ticked-box' approach. The public sector consensus seems to be that just mentioning the aspiration to implement gender mainstreaming is adequate proof of the state's commitment. Added to this, following a Cabinet reshuffle in 2001 and the reconfiguration of ministerial responsibilities, there is no longer direct accountability within government for benchmarks, targets or any other measure of the output of the mainstreaming process. This is a strategic issue that the WBG has done less lobbying on as the demand for its input has tended to be fairly policy-specific and driven by government demands and priorities.

Government may have embraced the idea that, if state practices are to be seen to be open and participatory, they need to include women. Further, they need to do so especially in areas where traditionally women have had little or no input into government policy and the decision-making processes of the state apparatus. Government has not yet got the message, however, that if they truly listen to women, they will need to institutionalise formal, sustained measures for conducting gender analyses of all policies and administrative processes. In other words, a sign that they have taken seriously the consultative voices of women's organisations like the WBG would be their getting down to the business of instituting an accountable gender mainstreaming system throughout the entire span of government business.

One of the major aims of the WBG has been to persuade government to produce a gender impact analysis of its revenue and expenditure. However, it has not been able to convince the Treasury or any other government departments of the need to do a gender audit of expenditure. This may be related to the lack of a dialogue with grassroots women's groups who typically put women's issues on the parliamentary agenda by pressuring MPs directly. Grassroots activists' emphasis on targeting MPs can create a political impetus for change rather than a purely bureaucratic one. WBG's contact with the policy-making process has largely been with senior public officials and a number of ministers by raising concerns relevant to their policy portfolios. Both points of emphasis are important, but could advance the gender agenda better if more cohesively pursued.

Another consideration is that the idea of gender audits or even gender mainstreaming is still not widely enough accepted among women's groups for it to become a cause around which they create political pressure. In the WBG's work on gender budgeting to date, much attention is understandably directed at the economic planners themselves. But public sector success in mainstreaming gender will depend in part on the capacities of stakeholders inside and outside the government sector to provide the oversight that supports them in, and commits them to, this task (St. Hill, 2001: 16). Perhaps, for all these reasons, future engagement with a wide cross section of UK women's groups will create a useful amalgamation of political activism and expert advocacy for the urgent application of these two crucial tools of gender analysis.

A more foundational challenge is to get the UK government to go beyond a half-hearted acknowledgement of the existence of vast quantities of women's unpaid labour, to creating social policies and economic incentives that recognise the value of this work and the importance of its redistribution between men and women, family and society. At present, this seems incompatible with the government's continuing emphasis on paid work as the major thrust of its welfare reform. Because the spending reductions at the heart of government welfare reforms are more concerned with reducing taxation and public expenditure than with gender equity, government is unlikely to relieve women of some of their care work by the general extension of public services or more generous benefits for the most vulnerable groups of women. The WBG has made strong representations on this score in the past and will no doubt continue to do so in the future. Already, government is beginning to pay at least lip service to these assertions by acknowledging women's double day in some of its official publications. There may be some room for optimism that, in terms of policy reform, rhetoric is preceding reality.

Future Opportunities

Despite a range of challenges, the future of the WBG in the UK looks bright. In conclusion, all that remains is to touch on some of the opportunities that exist at present and others which are unfolding.

The WBG is currently evolving to where leadership of the national debate on gender and government policy is not only desirable but essential if its work is to be used to further an understanding of female empowerment as an end in itself and not just a means to macro-economic goals decided on by government in isolation from women. To facilitate greater utilisation by government of gender analysis within its current frameworks will be no easy task as it will require external monitoring, internal capacity building, political will and considerable public resources. Increased levels of funding from a broader base of donors, coupled with a focus on the recent statement of intent to lead the national conversation on gender and macro-economic policy, should set the WBG well on the way to realising its potential.

In terms of the constant bugbear of funding, there are signs that many ethically minded corporations are willing to provide financial support to approaches that can provide them with a more diverse workforce and more gender-equitable working practices. Increasingly, large corporate players recognise that a more gender-equitable macroeconomic policy framework is an important prerequisite to developing the optimal workplace of the future. Many women's groups are wary that taking support from private companies may jeopardise their vision of independent action and that they may be co-opted. However, with advanced states aiming to function more and more like managerial corporations, this danger can as easily occur in the public sector as in the private. Suitable commercial entities need to be identified and targeted for collaboration as they can be invaluable supporters in lobbying a government that puts so much emphasis on employment within its modernisation agenda.

The WBG is already taking advantage of opportunities to engage in popular and media debates, including at the European level, on furthering the gender budgeting agenda. The recently constructed WBG website (www.wbg.org.uk/) presents one opportunity to play a more public role in emerging debates. The website is also a low-cost activity both in terms of members' time and communication costs.

Diversity and complexity are not areas that it has embraced fully in the past, despite a well-developed gender-class nexus. However, by building on its competence on women and poverty, the WBG is well placed to strategise with organisations working for economic empowerment on behalf of women whose gender identity intersects with those of race, ethnicity and culture. Like all other feminist vehicles for empowering women, gender budgeting will need a movement if it is to reap the successes it has the potential to claim.

References

Commission for Racial Equality (1997). *Ethnic Minority Women*. CRE, London.

Himmelweit S. (2000). *The Experience of UK Women's Budget Group.* Paper prepared for the International Workshop on Gender Auditing of Government Budgets. Rome, September.

Rake K. (2002). *Gender Budgets: The Experience of the UK Women's Budget Group.* Paper prepared for the Conference on "Gender Balance – Equal Finance". Basle, Switzerland, March.

St Hill D. (2001). *Out of the Annex and Into the Main Building: Mainstreaming Gender Analysis in Macro Economic Planning.* United Nations Economic Commission for Latin America and the Caribbean, Port of Spain, Trinidad, June.

About the Contributors

Debbie Budlender is a Principal Researcher at the Community Agency for Social Enquiry, a policy research NGO. She has been the overall coordinator and editor of the South African WBI since it began in 1995. She has worked in about twenty different countries, assisting international agencies, governments, parliaments and civil society partners with gender budget work.

Ngone Diop-Tine is an economist and a gender expert. She has been working in Rwanda since August 2001 as Gender Analyst Adviser to the Government of Rwanda under the United Kingdom's Department for International Development's (DFID) support programme to the country. It is in that capacity that she has been involved in the Rwanda Gender Budget Initiative (GBI), which she conceptualised.

Rona Fitzgerald is a Research Fellow at the European Policies Research Centre at the University of Strathclyde. She specialises in the analysis and development of tools for mainstreaming gender equality in the EU's regional policy and in public policy-making in Ireland and the UK.

Celia Flor is the Executive Director of DAWN and has been a city councillor since 1995. She has travelled all over the Philippines and to several other countries to share her experiences of transformative governance, gender advocacy and mainstreaming.

Morag Gillespie is the newly appointed Parliamentary Liaison and Development worker for the Engender Women's Budget Group (EWBG) in Scotland.

Guy Hewitt is a Senior Programme Officer in the Gender Section at the Commonwealth Secretariat, and programme manager of the Commonwealth GRB initiative. He advises Commonwealth governments on the implementation of gender-responsive budgets and also provides technical support to other intergovernmental organisations and developmental agencies.

Janine Hicks is the Director of the Provincial Parliamentary Programme (PPP), an advocacy and public participation NGO. Her background experience includes human rights NGO programme management, training, publications and materials development, and fund raising.

Helena Hofbauer is Executive Director of FUNDAR, a research centre dedicated to promoting democracy in Mexico, with a particular focus on applied budget analysis. FUNDAR has been part of the Mexican gender budget initiative since 2000, training diverse groups and analysing the gendered implications of the federal budget.

Andrea Lizares-Si has been President of DAWN since 1993 and was a practicing lawyer before she was appointed City Administrator in 2001. Aside from her involvement in gender advocacy, she has a Master of Divinity degree and loves to mountain-bike with her husband and seven children.

Ailsa McKay is a lecturer in economics at Glasgow Caledonian University. She is a member of the International Association of Feminist Economics (IAFFE) and has published articles on gender, work and poverty.

Angela O'Hagan is currently Director of Carers Scotland. She was previously Senior Policy Manager with EOC Scotland where she spent eight years developing practice on mainstreaming through national policy development, and transnational projects.

Rebecca Pearl is the Sustainable Development Programme Associate at the Women's Environment and Development Organization (WEDO), where she facilitates women's participation and advocacy in the United Nations World Summit on Sustainable Development. She helped UNIFEM-Andean Region launch the Programme on Women's Economic and Social Rights and gender-responsive budget initiatives.

Donna St Hill has been a member of the Women's Budget Group for four years and its first project manager. She has consulted and written extensively on gender and policy reform and was also the consultant for the Commonwealth Secretariat gender budget pilot in Barbados. She is completing a PhD on gender and macroeconomic policy.

Marian Sawer is head of the Political Science Programme in the Research School of Social Sciences at the Australian National University. She has a background as a policy practitioner and was responsible for the women's budget programme in the Australian Department of Foreign Affairs in the 1980s. She first analysed the Australian women's budget programme in her book *Sisters in Suits* (1990).

Yoon Jung Sook is currently co-Director of Korea WomenLink and the coordinator of the WomenLink local government gender budget programme. She is also a PhD candidate in the Women's Studies Department at Ewha Women's University. She joined WomenLink in 1987 as a full-time activist.

Lisa Vetten is the Gender Coordinator of the Centre for the Study of Violence and Reconciliation, where she is responsible for research, training and education, advocacy, policy and legislation development, and analysis in relation to gender and violence. She has worked in the area of violence against women since 1991.